PRAISE FOR *BREATH TO THE BONES*
ENDORSEMENTS

There is a movement afoot across the land. Churches that have languished for years are regaining hope that the risen Christ is not finished with them. Their future is bright. Spiritual territory that was once lost is being regained. The kingdom of God is advancing. Johnny Rumbough has been deeply involved in this church revitalization movement. In his new book, he shares the wisdom he has amassed through the years while helping numerous churches regain their health and vibrancy. You will be blessed and encouraged as you read it.

> **Richard Blackaby,** President
> Blackaby Ministries International
> *Developing A Christ-Centered Church,*
> *The Ways of God, Experiencing God.*

You will be hard-pressed to find someone who has personally walked more churches through renewal and revitalization with biblical clarity and observable success than Johnny Rumbough. Breath to Bones synthesizes a healthy blend of biblical foundation and contemporary wisdom for churches that are in need of spiritual renewal. Johnny's approach to church revitalization is gospel-centered, Spirit-filled, prayer-saturated, and missionally focused. Decades of faithfulness in church revitalization are born upon these pages.

> **Tony Wolfe,** Executive Director-Treasurer
> South Carolina Baptist Convention

Decades of missions, ministry, and experience come together in this book, *"Breath to the Bones"*: A Gospel Renaissance of the Gospel. Dr. Johnny Rumbough has lived this book and has creatively, thoughtfully, and painstakingly written a book that is certain to inspire and encourage pastors, other leaders of churches, and church members who want to see their churches be revived, revitalized, and encouraged to move forward in the mission of Christ. He cites numerous stories of churches he has helped to find their way to revitalization and renewal toward a fulfillment of their vision for the Lord's church. His insights, building on the motif of the valley of the dry bones in Ezekiel 37, are sure to bring out the creative thinking, planning, and visioning of pastors and other church leaders who deeply desire to see renewal come to their church. Both leaders in the church and small groups in a church will benefit alike from a study of this book. I have greatly appreciated the opportunity to read it, and it is already stirring up missional causes in my mind and heart. I heartily recommend this book to you

Charles Westbrook, Pastor, Pelion Baptist Church
Pelion, South Carolina

"Breath to the Bones" is a book that resonates deeply with the heart of any pastor, church leader, or believer who loves the local church. The stories Johnny Rumbough shares are not just snapshots of individual congregations; they represent a larger picture of what God is doing across our Southern Baptist family. Each chapter bears witness to the

lessons Johnny has learned as God has worked through him and through the life of each church. This book is a powerful reminder that God is faithful. He sustains His church, not by our strength or strategies, but by His will and purposes. Johnny's journey invites us to celebrate that truth, to be encouraged in our own ministries, and to look with renewed hope to the One who continues to breathe life into His people.

Lee Butler, Associational Mission Strategist
Lexington Baptist Association, Lexington, South Carolina

Johnny has always had a deep love for the local church and its leaders. He has invested much of his life in coming alongside struggling churches with a passion to see them return to vitality and effectiveness as God's people. Through the years, he has accumulated a variety of stories and experiences. In this book, he leverages those in practical ways that speak to the issues facing the local church and offer help and hope for their future. I commend Johnny's book to you as another valuable resource within the renewal and revitalization movement. If the church is to bring the truth of the Gospel to those we are called to serve, we must pay attention to those things that matter most, living with God's heart and on God's agenda.

Rick Fisher, Vice-President
Blackaby Ministries International

Decades of faithfulness and fruitfulness in church renewal work are packed into this short book. Johnny's wisdom and experience are remarkably valuable for any church pursuing renewal. This work is highly practical with practices that come from real world experiences. The stories provide hope for churches in across contexts. Whether you are a pastor, deacon, or church member, this work will encourage and equip you to pursue renewal in your church for God's glory and the good of your community.

Brandon Moore, Replant Specialist
North American Mission Board, SBC

"Breath to the Bones" has a central message to the church, the church member, and the church leader; that is woven together by seamless words that piece one honest message throughout: Renewal by the Spirit of God. If you are longing for God to breathe breath into you again, this is the book for you, but warning: It will challenge you and change you! This book is foundational for any church, individual, or pastor seeking renewal—it is a "must read!"

Jeff Powell, pastor, Green Hill Baptist Church
West Columbia, South Carolina

This relatively short book is packed with practical information and wise advice about church renewal. It provides an optimistic description of what God can do for dying churches and struggling church leaders, and illustrates such with descriptions of what God has done in various churches. The included questions help readers explore what needs to change in a congregation and in their own lives. *"Breath to the Bones"* has led me to depend more on the Holy Spirit's work in my life and in the life of the congregation I serve. It can help a church in almost any situation <u>breathe</u> again.

Ken Harmon, interim pastor, Northwood Baptist Church
Lexington, South Carolina

Johnny Rumbough is a gift from God to the Church. With razor-sharp clarity and profound insight, he shares a lifetime of wisdom and accumulated experience from his ministry alongside churches in need of God's help. Surgically applying deep truths from the Scripture and over two dozen case study stories, the author diagnoses and prescribes a variety of symptoms and solutions to current church diseases. He helps us, the readers, evaluate our own situation in light of the purifying fire of God's Word and thoughtful, practical applications. These short chapters, pithy statements, and reflection questions can stimulate hopeful thoughts and much needed action steps, if you will let them. Johnny is right: "Renewal begins when a congregation is willing to name what is broken, return to the Gospel, and pray for God to breathe life into His church again." *Breath to the Bones* is greatly needed in the Church today; I highly recommend you read this book.

Dr. David Jackson, Replant/Renewal Specialist
North American Mission Board, SBC
Author of *Falling in Love with Jesus (Again)*

BREATH
TO THE
BONES

A Gospel Renaissance of the Local Church

I0156929

DR. JOHNNY RUMBOUGH

Library of Congress Control Number: 2025921960

First Edition, 2025

Author's Note

*The twenty-five Church Stories shared in this book are true.
The names of the churches are entirely fictitious, except
two (maybe three ☺).*

With a grateful heart and deepest love,
I dedicate this Book...

To My Wife

Breathe! Breathe! Breathe! Those were my desperate words to my bride, Valerie English Rumbough, on the morning of May 14, 2023—Mother's Day—when she fell from our back deck onto the concrete below and went into cardiac arrest three times. I am profoundly grateful she heard my urgent pleas—and even more grateful God answered by filling her lungs with breath once again.

Today, she is a thriving Jesus follower, wife, mother, mother-in-law, and Nana.

To the Local Church

Breathe! Breathe! Breathe! is my plea to our Lord's Bride, to every local church, longing not just to survive, but to thrive—and bring God great glory.

CONTENTS

FOREWORD

My friend, you are about to embark on a journey into the heart of one of the most difficult and glorious works of God: the renewal of a church. If you are a pastor or a church leader, you may have picked up this book with a heavy heart, burdened by the decline you may have seen in your own congregation. You may be tired of looking back at faded memories and old trophies, and you are exhausted by the thought of trying to conjure up a new future for your church.

This book is not a silver bullet. You will not find quick-fix formulas or pragmatic strategies that bypass the hard work. What you will find, however, is a profound and hope-filled truth: Jesus has a plan for your church. The question is not what *your* plan is, but what is *His*? Our job is to come into obedience to His will, not the other way around.

I have wrestled with the very same question that so many of you have: "What about a dying church brings glory to God?" The answer, as I have concluded time and again, is simple: "Nothing". A church that closes its doors, in a community still desperate for the good news of Jesus, is a tragic testimony that robs God of the glory He deserves. When a church ceases to be salt and light, God's work appears irrelevant to a watching world.

But this story is not one of tragedy. It is a story of hope and resurrection. The same God who brought life out of a dead stump for Jesse's family is still in the business of bringing dead things back to life. He can—and is—

revitalizing dying churches all across North America in numbers we have never seen before.

This is a gospel work, an act of worship. It requires us to lay down our own agendas, preferences, and long-held traditions at the foot of the cross. We must repent of our pride and our need for control and embrace a humble, servant's heart. True revitalization comes when a church, prompted by a vision of a greater joy found in Christ, is willing to relinquish its own idols.

So what does the hard work of revitalization look like? My good friend and colleague Johnny Rombough reveals this truth in this book. Breathe to the Bones is born from a wealth of firsthand knowledge. Johnny brings the passion of a pastor and the strategy of a missionary in this book that reveals the inspiration and insight that our Lord had revealed to Johnny in his decades of serving the local church.

It's my pleasure to highly commend this book to all of you seeking to find Jesus' plan for your church. You will find this to be an indispensable tool written by someone who has a heart for the gospel, a heart for the local Church, and a heart for the Pastor.

Mark Clifton
Executive Director, Revitalization and Replant
North American Mission Board
September 10, 2025

Hebrews 12:1–2 – *"Therefore, since we are surrounded by so great a cloud of witnesses, let us also lay aside every weight, and sin which clings so closely, and let us run with endurance the race that is set before us, looking to Jesus, the founder and perfecter of our faith, who for the joy that was set before him endured the cross, despising the shame, and is seated at the right hand of the throne of God."*

Introduction

This book is written for everyone in the local church who longs to see their congregation thrive once again for the glory of God! *Consider asking your congregation to read this book prior to or as a part of your renewal.*

How to Use This Book

There's no single "right" way to read this book. You might choose to move through it from beginning to end, or you may prefer to take it one chapter at a time. At the close of each chapter, you'll find questions designed to help you think more deeply and apply what you've read.

For the greatest impact, invite others to join you. Gather a few friends, fellow church members, or ministry leaders, and read a chapter together. Talk through the questions, share your perspectives, and encourage one another as you explore what God might be saying to you and your church.

Breath to the Bones: A Gospel Renaissance of the Local Church

Why "Breath to the Bones?" Resurrection always begins in a grave—a place that seems lifeless, forgotten, and beyond hope. Yet this is where God's work often starts. He is not finished with His church. He still breathes, and where He breathes, bones rise…and life begins.

Why "Gospel Renaissance?" The Apostle Paul reminded the early believers that the Gospel is *"of first importance."* When that Gospel becomes the heartbeat of a renaissance — a true rebirth—within the local church, the result is a Spirit-driven resurrection. This is how a church moves from decline to vitality, stepping into a future that is thriving and bringing God great glory.

BREATH

TO THE

BONES

A Gospel Renaissance of the Local Church

The Graveyard Church

Chapter 1

The Graveyard Church

When the Gospel Is Gone, So Is Life

Key Text: Ezekiel 37:1
"The hand of the Lord was upon me, and He brought me out in the Spirit of the Lord and set me down in the middle of the valley; it was full of bones."

A Church Story: The "Graveyard" Church

The "Graveyard" Church once served a suburban neighborhood in a metropolitan area. "Welcome" was the actual name of the church. As the community's demographics shifted over time, families moved away, new families arrived, and longtime members felt increasingly uncertain about the future. Attendance declined, discouragement grew, and eventually the congregation made the painful decision to disband and disperse.

More than twenty years later, I drove past the location where the church once stood. The church was gone, but the roadside sign remained—its faded message still inviting people to a church that no longer existed. The sight led me to pull to the roadside. A wave of grief came over me as the thought formed in my heart: *"Welcome is no longer here."*

That moment reminded me why renewal is urgent—because every church has a choice: to fade into memory slowly or to breathe again by the Spirit of God for the glory of His Kingdom.

The Weight of the Valley

Let's be honest. Who would ask to be taken to a graveyard and be set down in the middle of the remains of what used to be alive? Not me and probably not you. And yet that's exactly where God placed the prophet in Ezekiel 37. Not in the beautiful sanctuary of a temple. Not in the holy seclusion of a mountaintop. Instead, God placed Ezekiel in an aged valley full of dry, brittle, lifeless bones.

The imagery is vivid—bones without flesh, scattered and sun-bleached from what appeared to be the outcome of a long-dead army. This wasn't the scene of a recent tragedy. It was the scene of long-standing loss. This graveyard had been forgotten, abandoned, and beyond human hope.

Yet the Spirit of God set Ezekiel down in the middle of this valley of bones. Not above it. Not as an observer. But in the middle of a sea of deadness, God placed him.

Are you connecting with this story on any level in your life? In your own personal spiritual life? In your current church's life?

Sadly, many feel they have been set down in the middle of a hopeless, lifeless valley. They wish they were in a thriving church with endless energy and life. A church where visible signs of vivacity are plentiful. A church where the sight of lost souls receiving Jesus as Savior and following His command to be baptized is normal. A church where disciples are being made, multiplied, and sent to advance the Gospel abroad—a church giving birth to new churches.

And that's where many pastors, leaders, and faithful members find themselves today—wishing their situation were different, but instead they are **in a valley of dry bones.**

Not in a mega-church staff meeting with creative teams and capital campaigns. But in a church that feels like it's been in decline for a generation. Where the bones of a once-thriving ministry are now the only thing left, and there, in the quiet, God asks a question:

"Son of man, can these bones live?" (Ezekiel 37:3a)

The Courage to Be Honest

It takes courage to be honest about your reality. It takes even more courage to admit that you are, by all appearances, currently sitting in a graveyard.

Notice, Ezekiel did not deny where he was. He didn't try to sugarcoat the scene. He didn't try to skip ahead to the good part. He let the Lord lead him back and forth among the bones, inspecting them, absorbing the reality.

THE FIRST STEP OF RENEWAL IS HONESTY. Before embarking on strategy, plans, vision casting, worship redesign, or community outreach campaigns, it's essential to have an honest and humble recognition of where you currently are.

For many, honesty is too painful to face. The signs are hard to admit—an aging membership with no young families, prayerless meetings, worship that feels dry and lifeless, a community that no longer knows your church's name, conflicts that were never fully healed, and leaders who are exhausted and no longer inspired.

Yet honesty—painful as it is—is the starting point of renewal. Jesus said to His disciples, *"...the truth will set you free"* (John 8:32b). God does not work with illusions; He works with truth.

When God asked Ezekiel, *"Son of man, can these bones live?"* (Ezekiel 37:3a), the prophet gave the only wise answer:

"O Lord God, you know." Ezekiel 37:3b

Ezekiel wasn't dodging the question—he was confessing the truth. His words reflected a heart of surrender and the recognition that the One who gives life is the only One who could restore the life that was lost.

Renewal begins when you are willing to be brutally honest about where you are—even if that place feels like a spiritual graveyard.

HONESTY IS A SERIOUS LOOK IN THE MIRROR. Before a pastor, a congregation, or a church can move forward, there must be a hard, prayerful look in the mirror.

Ask yourself: What do I see—or not see? Do I have the courage to own what I see? Am I blaming others for what is mine to own?

HOPE GROWS WHERE HONESTY LIVES. No pastor, no people, no church can be revived without the breath of God. And when God breathes life, He gives life. He does not merely resuscitate—He recreates. He doesn't return you to the "good old days," but moves you toward a brand-new future of significance for His glory.

From a Vibrant Church to Dry Bones

My call to the Gospel ministry came on April 20, 1975. Over the course of these five decades, I have had the privilege of serving many great churches. I have seen them in seasons of strength—and, sadly, in seasons of struggle. When a church allows the Gospel to drift from center to side, it usually doesn't begin with a catastrophe. More often, it begins quietly, almost imperceptibly. A once-vibrant church slowly begins to lose its clarity, passion, and power, causing it to gradually slip into a decline.

Vitality gives way to routine. Purpose slips into memory. What was once alive with mission becomes hollow with motion.

This drifting of Gospel-centeredness rarely comes from one dramatic decision. Instead, it comes from a series of small shifts—subtle on their own but devastating over time. Left unaddressed, they lead a church not just into stagnation, but into a valley of spiritual dryness—and, eventually, death.

Most churches don't collapse. They erode. The decline is slow, subtle, and sometimes even unnoticed until it's too late.

Some common causes of this slow, silent fade include the following:

1. Mission Drift

One of the most common deadly drifts is **mission drift**. The term, popularized by Peter Greer and Chris Horst in their 2014 book *Mission Drift*, describes how faith-based organizations gradually lose sight of their original purpose. The local church, too, can forget why She exists. The Great Commission becomes, as some have said, the great assumption. Outreach recedes. Ministries and focus shift inward. What once pulsed with mission becomes a comfortable echo chamber unrealizing their presence in a valley of lifeless dry bones, blind to the very reason it was birthed.

2. Leadership Fatigue

Then come the unsuspecting, lethal consequences of **leadership fatigue**. Passionate pastors and ministry teams, once aflame with vision, find themselves drained and tired. Tired on the inside and outside. The pressures of ministry without Sabbath, support, or fresh vision weigh the leadership down. What began as a calling begins to feel like a chore. Sermons lose their fire. Ministry becomes maintenance. Risk is replaced by routine, and the local church—though still active—runs on the fumes of yesterday's passion. This isn't just burnout; it's the slow surrender to survival mode, often leading to ministry departures. And when leadership is weary, the church cannot breathe deeply. It cannot dream. Fatigue dulls discernment, chokes joy, and suffocates vision.

A recent study by Lifeway Research (June 2025), focusing on evangelical and Black Protestant pastors, found that 1.2 percent departed the pastorate annually for reasons other than retirement or death, meaning roughly 1 in 100 pastors exit the ministry each year.

According to Guidestone Financial Resources using the Barna Group as a "The State of Pastors" resource stated 65 percent of a select group surveyed report loneliness, 22 percent rate their physical well-being as "below average" or "poor," 59 percent do not practice the Sabbath weekly with their families, and 79 percent say they are "sometimes" or "frequently" emotionally or mentally exhausted.

When pastors or teams carry too much for too long, without vision, without sabbath, and without support, they burn out. What remains is maintenance, not ministry.

3. Generational Disconnect

A **generational disconnect** quietly erodes the future. Younger believers—eager to serve and lead—often find themselves without a place or a voice. Their ideas are dismissed, their presence is unnoticed, and their potential remains untapped. And so, they slip away—not in protest, but from the absence of connection to their purpose. The pews grow older. The songs feel distant. The culture stays still. And without intentional mentoring, listening, and sharing of leadership, the baton remains unpassed, and the next leg of the race falters before it begins. Books like *Growing Young[1]*, *Autopsy of a Deceased Church[2]*, and *Didn't See It Coming[3]* shine light on these very patterns.

If younger generations don't find a place, voice, or purpose in the church, their absence will grow louder over time.

4. Unaddressed Sin or Conflict

Some wounds go deep—**unaddressed sin or conflict** that never fully heal. A moral failure was swept under the rug. Gossip that splintered trust. A painful split that left scar tissue in its wake. When these moments are not acknowledged and addressed, they don't disappear—they become embedded in the culture. People stop speaking up. Leaders walk on eggshells. The church limps along, afraid to hope again. True healing requires more than time. It demands truth-telling, repentance, forgiveness, and Spirit-led reconciliation. Until then, pain poisons the possibility.

Lingering tension, past church splits, or moral failures create spiritual scar tissue. Without healing, the church limps instead of running.

5. Cultural Isolation

And finally, there's the pull of **cultural isolation**—where a church is unsure how to relate to the world around it. Some try to mimic the culture so closely that they lose their spiritual voice. Others retreat from the world entirely, forfeiting influence and mission. But the Gospel was never meant to be echoed or hidden.

Faithful presence means engaging culture with courage—rooted in truth, grounded in grace, alive in the Spirit. A local church that silences or isolates herself—either through imitation or withdrawal—misses the very places where the Good News is needed most.

Each of these is like a blow to the bones—separating them further, drying them out, and making them seem beyond recovery.

Five Questions to Ask Before Renewal

Every church has lifeless, dry bones. Not just the obvious signs of decline—empty pews, aging buildings, shrinking budgets—but the deeper, invisible fractures that quietly sap the life from within. These "bones" are the remnants of what once was: ministries that thrived, leaders who led, moments of Spirit-filled momentum. But over time, without breath, they have dried out. They may still be present, but they are no longer alive.

These bones might be programs that no longer serve a purpose but still demand time and energy. They might be outdated structures that resist change. They could be wounds—conflicts unresolved, grief unspoken, trauma unhealed. Sometimes, the bones are sacred cows: traditions that are loved more than the mission itself.

To begin the journey of renewal, you must first name what is lifeless. This requires deep, prayerful reflection— asking the hard questions that expose what lies beneath the surface. The following probing questions are worth asking.

1. What past strength has now become a burden?

Perhaps a ministry or method once used powerfully by God has become an idol. Maybe you're holding onto what worked in the past, even though it no longer yields results.

2. What unspoken grief is your church carrying?

Local churches mourn too—loss of members, leadership failures, moral collapse, painful splits. What has been buried beneath the surface, never named, never grieved?

3. Where has vision stalled or been lost entirely?

Is your church merely maintaining its status quo, rather than moving forward? Has the sense of divine purpose grown foggy or even forgotten?

4. What assumptions about "how church should be" are holding you back?

Are you locked into certain styles, schedules, or structures simply because "that's the way it's always been done"? What if those assumptions are more cultural than biblical?

5. What might God be asking you to lay down before He can raise up something new?

Renewal often begins with relinquishment. Is there something you're holding onto that God is asking you to release—so He can do something fresh?

These questions don't condemn—they clarify. Clarity confronts us with the need to be honest about our current reality, which is the first step toward renewal.

Coming to grips with them is not easy. It requires humility, honesty, and a willingness to enter the valley. Only *bones* acknowledged by God can rise to become a great army. And when you think things are too far gone, maybe it's precisely the *time and place* God decides to give breath to the bones once again.

What are the bones in your church?

A Church Story: The "Wedding" Church

For decades, The "Wedding" Church was a thriving congregation in an established part of the city. In recent years, however, attendance had steadily declined—from more than 100 active members to fewer than 50. When their beloved pastor unexpectedly passed away, the congregation was left grieving and even more uncertain about the future.

God provided by leading The "Wedding" Church to call a seasoned interim pastor to shepherd them. After helping the church congregation walk through their grief, he guided them to face a painful yet honest reality: the church was dying. At their request, I led The "Wedding" Church through a renewal process that helped the congregation, mostly senior adults, see the need to reach young families.

The process led to a partnership with a relatively new church plant, thriving with young couples and children. Realizing they needed each other, the two congregations merged into one. **They wedded.** Today, the replanted "Wedding" Church is thriving with a mixture of senior adults, young adults, and children worshiping together.

Their story reminds us that even in the painful seasons of decline, God can write a new chapter of renewal when His people are willing to embrace change for the sake of the Gospel.

Reflection Questions

1. Where in your church do you sense the breath of God is missing?

_____

_____

2. Are there things you are trying to prop up?

_____

_____

3. Are you willing to walk in the valley—and wait for His breath?

_____

_____

Closing Prayer

Jesus, You are the center of everything. Forgive us for the ways we've drifted. Breathe life into us again—not through our strength, but through Your finished work. Let the Gospel not only save us, but also sustain us. Amen.

Breath to the Bones

Chapter 2

The Gospel-Centered Church

Renewal Always Starts with the Gospel

Key Text: 1 Corinthians 15:3–4
"For I delivered to you as of first importance what I also received: that Christ died for our sins in accordance with the Scriptures, that He was buried, that He was raised on the third day in accordance with the Scriptures."

A Church Story: The "Gospel" Church

You never forget the moment a church gasps for breath again.

The "Gospel" Church was once a thriving congregation, sending out pastors and missionaries and serving as a beacon in the community. Over time, as the membership aged, pastoral transitions and hardships took their toll. Attendance declined sharply, and morale weakened.

When their leaders reached out for help, the church agreed to enter a renewal process. I'll never forget a midweek gathering when only 18 people sat together in a side room of a sanctuary that once seated over 300. They were faithful, yet weary saints refusing to give up, leaders quietly wondering if God was finished with their church.

After the closing prayer, a young woman approached me with a trembling voice and downcast eyes. "I feel so guilty," she whispered. "How can I be forgiven?" There was no music, no altar call—just the sacred sound of a lost soul being found. Tears filled the room as one of the older women whispered through her own sobs, *"God is still breathing here."* In that moment, renewal began—not with a program, but with the Gospel breaking through the silence of a weary church.

In time, the congregation entered a replanting partnership with a sister church. Through humility, repentance, prayer, and the preaching of God's Word, the Spirit of God breathed life into The "Gospel" Church once again. Today, the congregation is experiencing a fresh season of renewal and growth, with new believers being added to their number.

The first sound after silence was the sound of resurrection. Their story reminds us that renewal begins not with crowds returning, but when even one soul gasps for grace and a weary church remembers why the church exists.

A Warning for the Modern Church

The following verses remind us there is a vast difference between mere assembly and true awakening:

"Then he said to me, 'Prophesy over these bones, and say to them, O dry bones, hear the Word of the Lord. Thus says the Lord God to these bones: Behold, I will cause breath to enter you, and you shall live. And I will lay sinews upon you, and will cause flesh to come upon you, and cover you with skin, and put breath in you, and you shall live, and you shall know that I am the Lord.' So I prophesied as I was commanded. And as I prophesied, there was a sound, and behold, a rattling, and the bones came together, bone to its bone. And I looked, and behold, the sinews on them, and flesh had come upon them, and skin had covered them. But there was no breath in them." Ezekiel 37:4-8

In these verses, God commands Ezekiel to prophesy to the bones, and something miraculous happens. The bones begin to rattle. They come together. Tendons and flesh appear. Bodies reassemble. **But these bones are still not alive**.

The lifeless dry bones form before the breath. Structure without Spirit. Body without wind. Bones without life.

This is a critical warning for the modern church: you can organize a crowd without ever inviting the breath of God. It's entirely possible to host excellent services, preach well-crafted sermons, play modern worship music, maintain engaging social media, and even enjoy financial stability— yet remain spiritually lifeless.

Form alone is not revival. Strategy without the Spirit is scaffolding without a building.

This is the danger of cosmetic church renewal—changing what is seen while neglecting what is unseen. Working to organize an assembled crowd without an awakening is futile. You can't schedule breath. We can only seek it.

What Is the Gospel?

The Gospel is not a vague idea about love or goodness. It is a **specific announcement** of what God has done in and through Christ Jesus.

Before time began, the eternal God created us to know Him and to live with Him forever. But sin entered the world and broke that perfect relationship, separating every one of us from our Creator. Because of His great love, God Himself came to us—Jesus Christ, the Son of God. He was born as a man, lived a sinless life, suffered, and died on the cross for our sins. On the third day, He rose from the dead in a real, physical body. His disciples saw Him, touched His scars, and even ate with Him to prove He was alive. After appearing to many, He ascended into heaven and promised that one day He will return. Yet His death and resurrection do not save us automatically. Each of us must **turn from our sins and repent, inviting Jesus into our hearts**. When we **receive Jesus into our hearts as Lord and Savior**, trusting in His finished work on the cross, His sacrifice cleanses us and restores us to God. Those who repent and believe will share eternal life with Him in the new heaven and new earth when

He comes again—a joyful reunion with all who belong to Christ.

The Gospel is THE GOOD NEWS for nonbelievers to receive. The Gospel is THE GOOD NEWS for believers to share. You don't grow past the Gospel. You grow *in* the Gospel. The Gospel is the life of the believer and the breath God breathes into the local church.

Gospel Renaissance of the Local Church

The "breath" in Ezekiel's vision represents the Spirit of God. In Hebrew, the word is *ruach,* meaning breath, wind, or spirit. When God says, *"Prophesy to the breath"* (Ezekiel 37:9), He is calling Ezekiel to speak not just to the bones, but to heaven itself—to call down life, to plead for God's presence, to invite what no human effort can accomplish.

For the local church today, seeking breath means praying with desperation. It means confessing sin. It means preaching Christ. It means creating space for the Spirit to move. It means calling out to the heavens for God to breathe life into half-hearted, lifeless gatherings.

True renewal is not about tweaking systems. It is about welcoming the breath of God back into the lungs of the local church. The Apostle Paul tells the Corinthians to keep the Gospel of *"first importance:"*

"For I delivered to you as of first importance what I also received: that Christ died for our sins in accordance with the Scriptures, that He was buried, that He was raised on the

third day in accordance with the Scriptures." 1 Corinthians 15:3–4

He didn't say the Gospel was helpful. He said it was **of first importance**. This means the Gospel is not just the entry point into Christianity—it's the atmosphere in which all of Christianity is lived. It is the air the Church breathes.

Renewal always starts with the Word. When the Word is obeyed and the Gospel is *"of first priority"* (at the center), the local church experiences:

1. Power — As Romans 1:16 declares, *"It is the power of God for salvation to everyone who believes."* The Gospel is not just inspiring—it is transforming. It replaces self-help with supernatural help. It brings dead things to life.

2. Unity — Only the Gospel has the power to bring together people from every background—sinners and saints, skeptics and seekers. Galatians 3:28 reminds us that we are all one in Christ. Where the Gospel reigns, unity thrives over division, love over preference.

3. Joy — Psalm 51:12 says, *"Restore to me the joy of your salvation."* The Gospel awakens the deepest kind of joy— joy not rooted in circumstances, but in Christ. It brings back music to our worship, warmth to our community, and wonder to our gatherings.

4. Mission — The Gospel is not only good news to be believed—it is good news to be shared. Jesus' command to *"make disciples of all nations"* (Matthew 28:19-20) becomes our joy-filled calling. A Gospel-centered church doesn't just survive—it multiplies.

5. Purpose in Gathering — Acts 2 paints a vibrant picture of a church shaped by the Gospel. They devoted themselves to the apostles' teaching, fellowship, prayer, and breaking of bread. The Gospel infused every gathering with meaning and every moment with mission.

Without the Gospel, even the most beautiful church structures lose their life. **No Gospel. No Life.**

You can have a stunning building, a skilled staff, thriving programs, a rich history, and a strong budget—but if the Gospel is not central, it's only a matter of time before the church begins to die.

BUT HERE'S THE GOOD NEWS: **God still breathes into dry bones.** And when the Gospel is restored to its rightful place—not just as a motto, but as the message and the lifeblood—everything changes. Life returns. Unity returns. Mission returns. Joy returns.

A Church Story: The "Renewed" Church

The interim pastor urged his congregation, *"You need to contact the local Baptist association and ask them about a Futuring Process they are leading churches through."* He was so convinced of its importance that he warned the church leaders he might leave if they did not pursue it.

Soon after, I received a call from one of the leaders: *"Our interim pastor keeps telling us we need to contact the association about a Futuring Process. Will you meet with us and tell us more?"* I agreed, and afterwards, the church chose to begin the journey.

What followed was more than a program—it was a spiritual experience. God stirred a movement within the church. When the process was complete and a new pastor was called, the momentum grew, as the pastor faithfully preached God's Word and led the congregation in evangelism.

As a result, The "Renewed" Church began to grow through Gospel-centered outreach, intentional discipleship, and the power of God's Word proclaimed. Their story reminds us that renewal begins when a church is willing to humble itself, seek guidance, and allow the Spirit to breathe new life again.

Seven Signs of a Gospel-Centered Church

What does a Gospel-centered church look like—not just in theology, but in everyday life? Indeed, it's more than just having the right words on a website or doctrinal statements on paper. I once heard a friend say, "It's creating a vibrant culture where grace is experienced—preached with conviction, sung with joy, shared with love, and lived with authenticity."

The following are seven signs of a Gospel-centered local church.

1. Christ Is Preached Clearly and Consistently

The message of Jesus' death, burial, and resurrection is not just mentioned—it is central. Every sermon, study, and strategy points back to the finished work of Christ and the grace of God.

The pulpit becomes a sacred space where the redemptive story of Christ shines through every passage—whether in Genesis or Revelation. Sermons connect the head and the heart. They don't just teach; they transform. Every message helps us see more of Jesus and remember how much we need Him, stirring deep affection and renewed commitment.

"We preach Christ crucified..." 1 Corinthians 1:23

2. Grace Shapes the Culture

Instead of guilt, shame, or performance, the tone of the church reflects mercy, humility, and second chances. People are welcomed, not because they have it all together, but because Jesus does.

Relationships are real, sincere, and rooted in Christ. People walk together through life's highs and lows, carrying each other with compassion. In this kind of church, everyone belongs—not because they have it all together, but because Jesus holds them together. Accountability is offered with love, and vulnerability is met with understanding. It's a family, not a crowd.

"Where sin increased, grace abounded all the more."
Romans 5:20

3. Repentance and Transformation Are Normal

The Gospel invites people to come as they are—but not to stay that way. Confession, repentance, and spiritual growth are expected and celebrated as part of ongoing renewal.

People are free to be honest because the cross has already covered their sin. Grace creates a safe space for healing, restoration, and fresh starts. Repentance isn't rare—it's refreshing. Transparency is met with kindness, not judgment. Forgiveness is celebrated, and lives are changed.

"Be transformed by the renewing of your mind..." –
Romans 12:2

4. Unity Is Rooted in Christ, Not Comfort

Diversity is embraced because the Gospel unites people across backgrounds, generations, and races. It is Christ—not politics, traditions, or styles—that holds the church together.

"...You are all one in Christ Jesus..." Galatians 3:28

5. Mission Flows from Identity

A Gospel-centered church doesn't just attend services—She lives "sent". Evangelism, disciple-making, and community engagement are natural expressions of being transformed by grace.

In a Gospel-centered church, every member sees themselves as "sent." The Great Commission isn't reserved for a few—it's lived out by all. The church becomes a launching pad, sending people into neighborhoods, schools, workplaces, and nations with the Good News. Hearts ignited by the Gospel naturally overflow in sharing it—near and far.

"Go therefore and make disciples of all nations..."
Matthew 28:19

6. Worship Is Centered on the Cross

Singing is not about performance but about praise. Worship exalts Jesus, not personalities. The Gospel fuels both reverence and joy, rooted in awe of who God is and what He has done.

It's not about impressing anyone—it's about meeting with the living Christ. Whether the music is contemporary, traditional, or a blend of both, the focus is always the same: beholding the beauty of Jesus. People sing with passion because they are overwhelmed by grace. The question is no longer, "Did I enjoy that song?" but "Did I see Christ more clearly?"

"Worthy is the Lamb who was slain..." Revelation 5:12

7. The Church Breathes the Gospel Together

Every ministry, from kids to seniors, from hospitality to outreach, is saturated with the Gospel. It's not a department or a topic—it's the air the church breathes.

Discipleship is not a one-time class or a short-term program—it's a continual transformation into the likeness of Christ. Rooted in Scripture and lived out in community, spiritual growth is nurtured with care. The church becomes a place where people flourish—not because of pressure, but because of God's presence. Love for Jesus deepens, love for others expands, and passion for His mission grows.

> *"...continue in the faith, stable and steadfast, not shifting*
> *from the hope of the gospel..."*
> Colossians 1:23

Ultimately, everything in a Gospel-centered church flows from and points back to Jesus—His finished work, His present power, and His coming kingdom. The result is not just better programs or more activity. The result is life. Real breath. Real joy. Real transformation. Because where the Gospel is central, the local church doesn't just function— She flourishes. She comes alive.

Six Signs of Gospel Displacement

One of the quietest tragedies in the life of a local church is knowing that the Gospel is displaced—it's no longer Gospel-centered. It typically isn't rebellion, but replacement. The message of Jesus is still spoken, but no longer central. It's on the website, in the doctrinal statement, and even mentioned in sermons, but it's no longer the heartbeat of the church.

The slide is almost always unintentional. No one stands up and says, "Let's move Jesus over to the margins." It happens subtly, gradually. Good things become focus things. Preferences take precedence over presence. Ministry becomes motion. And the cross moves out of focus.

So how do you know when it's happened? You begin to see the signs. Consider the following:

1. Worship slides from sacred encounter to scripted event.

The goal becomes smooth transitions, polished teams, and crowd engagement—not meeting with the living God. People often evaluate worship based on the setlist or sound system rather than their heart's surrender. The sanctuary becomes a stage, and the congregation becomes critics. When presence is replaced with performance, worship loses its wonder.

2. Preaching loses its edge when it stops pointing to Jesus.

Sermons may still be practical, clever, even inspiring—but they aren't transformational. The pulpit becomes a platform for moral advice, life improvement, or cultural commentary. Instead of leading people to the foot of the cross, messages start leading them to try harder, do better, fix themselves. But Christianity isn't a self-help system. It's a rescue mission. And without Jesus at the center, preaching becomes lifeless.

3. Church calendar may be full, but spiritual depth is shallow.

Events are held every week, but there are few spaces for real disciple-making. The local church becomes a place to attend, not a community to belong to. People are seen as volunteers, not brothers and sisters. Leaders feel busy, but not fruitful. In Gospel-centered churches, relationships drive the ministry. When the Gospel is displaced, relationships are replaced by rosters.

4. Keeping people happy starts to matter more than helping people grow.

Leaders begin to tiptoe around hard conversations, fearing they might offend. Difficult truths get softened. Conviction is avoided for the sake of keeping peace. But unity without truth is just artificial harmony. When control replaces conviction, the church might appear calm on the surface—but underneath, she is spiritually gasping. Holiness is traded for harmony, but it's a harmony without health.

5. The culture grows heavy, guarded, and exhausting.

People serve from obligation, not from overflow. Confession becomes rare. Transparency feels dangerous. The unspoken rule becomes: "Keep it together." When grace is not central, guilt quietly moves in. People begin to believe God loves them more when they do more. But the Gospel says the opposite: Christ's love is not earned—it's given. When grace fades, fear fills the gap. And the church becomes a place of performance, not freedom.

6. Eventually, energy turns inward. Vision shrinks.

The driving question becomes: "How do we keep this going?" instead of "Where is God calling us to go?" Focus shifts to survival, not surrender. Programs are preserved out of habit. Budgets are managed to maintain the status quo. And the once-burning question—"Who still needs to hear the Good News?"—is rarely asked. When mission fades, the church may still be busy, but she is no longer breathing.

The bottom line? When the Gospel is no longer central, the local church may still function—but she loses her life. Like a body disconnected from its breath, the forms may remain, but the Spirit fades.

But here's the hope: the Gospel is not gone. It's waiting to be brought back to the center. And when it is—when Jesus is exalted again, when grace is not assumed but adored—life begins to return. Breath fills the lungs of the church again.

Renewal doesn't begin with a program. It starts with a Person. Not a new method, but the old message—Christ crucified, risen, and reigning.

How to Lead Back to Gospel-Centeredness

Leading a local church back to Gospel-centeredness may be the hardest—and most beautiful—part of church renewal.

You can't simply stand up and declare, "We're going to be Gospel-centered now," and expect instant transformation. Gospel renewal doesn't happen by announcement—it happens by immersion. It's not just taught from the pulpit; it's modeled in the trenches. It takes time. It takes tears. It takes repentance. And it takes resolve.

Take heart: what begins with one surrendered leader can ripple through an entire congregation. You may be the spark.

If you want your church to breathe again, start by leading them back to the very source of life—the Gospel of Jesus Christ.

1. Preach the Gospel to yourself first.

Before you preach it to your people, preach it to your own soul—every day. Don't lead from a place of theological theory—lead from a place of personal transformation. Let the cross wreck you and restore you. Let grace not only forgive your past but rewire your motives. You cannot lead others into Gospel freedom if you are still living in a mode of performance, pressure, or pride. Ask yourself honestly: Is the Gospel good news to me—today? When the Gospel becomes your breath, it will naturally become your message.

2. Be willing to repent publicly and humbly.

One of the most powerful things a leader can say is, "I missed it." If you've led from fear instead of faith, from control instead of conviction, from effort instead of grace—own it. Your people don't need a perfect leader. They need a repentant one. Public repentance from the pulpit—done with humility, not theatrics—opens the door for the whole church to start fresh. It models what a Gospel-shaped culture looks like: honesty, brokenness, and hope. Let the first step back to the Gospel be marked by the Gospel itself—grace for leaders and grace for the whole body.

3. Make the Gospel visible again.

Don't just tell people about the Gospel—show them. Help your church see the Gospel, not just hear about it. Celebrate baptisms with joy and a clear explanation. Walk through the meaning of communion with reverence and clarity. Share real-life stories of salvation, restoration, and healing. Invite people to share their stories about how grace has transformed their lives. Let worship and Sunday gatherings radiate Gospel hope. When people see the Gospel in action, it moves from concept to reality. It becomes personal. It becomes powerful.

Note: One church records each baptism and replays the videos throughout the year—sometimes more than once— during Sunday morning services. It's a powerful reminder to the congregation of God's saving work and a celebration that keeps the joy of those moments alive.

4. As you lead forward, retrain and rebuild your leadership culture.

Don't assume your staff, deacons, or lay leaders fully understand what it means to be Gospel-centered. Many have been trained in systems, management, or ministry technique—but not in Gospel fluency. Walk with them. Read with them. Pray with them. Teach them how the Gospel affects leadership, decision-making, conflict, and communication. Give them room to wrestle. Give them language to grow. A Gospel-shaped church must first have Gospel-shaped leaders.

5. Pray for Gospel renewal relentlessly.

Renewal is not accomplished by sheer willpower. It is the work of the Spirit. And the Spirit moves through prayer. Call the church to pray. Call leaders to fast. Fill the sanctuary with prayers not for better services, but for spiritual awakening. Pray that hearts would burn again with affection for Christ. Pray that the Spirit would breathe on dry bones and cause them to rise. When Gospel renewal is the true focus of our prayers, God often responds in ways we never could have orchestrated.

6. Let the Gospel shape your decision-making.

Renewal isn't just about changing what we do—it's about changing why we do it. As a leader, begin filtering every major decision through this question: "Does this help us proclaim, embody, or advance the Gospel?" Budgets should reflect Gospel priorities, not just institutional maintenance. Stewarding resources isn't about survival—it's about sending. Events should have a purpose beyond the activity itself. Fellowship should be intentional. Outreach should be invitational. Nothing should be done "just because we always have." Personnel decisions must consider spiritual maturity, Gospel fluency, and alignment with the mission—not just talent or tenure. Programs should be evaluated regularly, and if they don't serve the mission, they must be reworked or released—with grace.

In time, the Gospel becomes the lens through which every decision is made—not just on Sunday, but every day. And this begins to shape a new culture: a Gospel-centered culture, not one focused on comfort or tradition, but on the mission of Christ.

A Church Story: The "Ridge" Church

When the longtime pastor of 35 years at The "Ridge" Church, located in a fast-growing suburban community, prepared to retire, he reached out seeking a healthy way to transition. This was deeply meaningful to me, since The "Ridge" Church was the church where I came to faith, was baptized, and was licensed to the ministry.

After meeting with him and the leadership, it became clear this was the right moment for the congregation to walk through a renewal process.

Though The "Ridge" Church was a healthy church, its numbers were slowly declining, and the danger of settling into routine was real. The renewal process helped them see that what they needed most was not simply a smooth transition, but a fresh awakening to the Gospel—the same Gospel that had carried them for generations.

As they prayed, sought God's Word, and re-centered their mission on Christ, the Spirit of God stirred new life within them. The retiring pastor finished well, passing the baton with grace, and the church stepped forward with renewed vision.

Today, The "Ridge" Church is thriving, marked by Gospel faithfulness and a fresh expectancy for the future.

Their story reminds us that Gospel awakening is not only for struggling churches, but for every church seeking to remain alive to the Spirit of God and postured to bring Him great glory.

Reflection Questions

1. In what ways has your church drifted from Gospel centrality?

_____

_____

2. What would it look like for your church to make the Gospel visible, audible, and experienced again?

_____

_____

3. Are there programs, phrases, or habits you need to reevaluate through a Gospel lens? (i.e. personal, family, work, church)

_____

_____

Closing Prayer

Jesus, You are the center of everything. Forgive us for the ways we've drifted. Breathe life into us again—not through our strength, but through Your finished work. Let the Gospel not only save us, but also sustain us. Amen.

Chapter 3

Courageous Confession

Facing the Truth About Where You Are

Key Text: Revelation 2:4-5
"But I have this against you, that you have abandoned the love you had at first. Remember therefore from where you have fallen; repent, and do the works you did at first."

A Church Story: The "Dusty" Church

The "Dusty" Church, located in a rural community, was known for being "friendly, traditional, and faithful." Banners and awards are appropriately placed, honoring seasons of past achievement. But during a pastoral transition, when I asked the leadership what God was presently doing among them, hope flickered in their eyes—yet few words followed.

They were not resistant; they were only honest. Faithfulness had become routine. Tradition had hardened into sediment. A layer of spiritual dust had quietly settled over their gatherings.

But God was not finished. As the church entered a season of renewal, prayer began to stir their hearts, and the

Gospel reclaimed its rightful place at the center. Soon, worship grew stronger, new leaders emerged, and members began stepping forward in fresh obedience to Christ. The church was awakening.

Today, The "Dusty" Church is no longer preserving memories but living on mission—a congregation alive for the glory of God.

Their story reminds us that every church must choose: to settle for survival, or to experience Gospel awakening through the renewing power of God's Spirit.

No church plans to lose its fire. It simply stops noticing the dust.

The Kindness of Christ in Confrontation

In Revelation 2, Jesus addresses the church at Ephesus—a congregation known for its theological soundness, sharp discernment, and steady endurance. On the surface, they were doing everything right. They had the truth, they recognized false teachers, and they didn't grow weary in doing good. But then Jesus says something devastatingly honest: *"You have abandoned the love you had at first."*

It's not a harsh rebuke. It's a holy piercing—a moment of divine confrontation not meant to destroy, but to summon them back to the Gospel.

This is the kindness of Christ. He doesn't ignore what's good, but neither does He excuse what's missing. He names the drift. He pierces through the performance and exposes the heart.

And this is where renewal truly begins.

Before renewal can come, a response to Jesus' invitation to repent must begin. We must repent of the subtle ways love has cooled, even while structure remains. We must repent of allowing the layers of nostalgia of past "glory days" to become an accepted substitute for a love that invites us to grow deeper in the Gospel.

We must repent of the clutter of comfort, the routines that make us feel secure but have no breath of the Spirit in them.

This kind of invitation doesn't come through strategic planning or the launch of new ministries. It comes when we accept God's call to truth and repentance, when we hear the voice of Jesus, not just as a critique, but as a calling. A loving confrontation from the One who walks among the lampstands, longing for His Church to return—not just to doctrine, but to devotion.

Renewal doesn't start with adding more things to the calendar. It begins with remembering what we've left behind—and, through repentance, returning to the One who first loved us.

Don't Let Dust Settle on Your Gospel

Dust is not evil. It's not an enemy. It's simply evidence— evidence that something has been left undisturbed for too long.

There are too many stories characteristic of dust settling on the Gospel. It accumulates slowly and quietly. It doesn't announce itself. When the wind of God's movement is no longer welcomed or expected, it settles. And by the time we notice it, it has often become part of the scenery.

Consider the following ways dust may settle in your heart, your life, your church.

1. Dust gathers when we stop asking hard questions.

When we no longer evaluate the spiritual fruit of our programs and ministries, we risk continuing for the sake of routine rather than renewal. Activities multiply, but transformation stalls.

2. Dust settles when methods matter more than mission.

We cling to familiar ways not because they still bear fruit, but because they feel safe. In doing so, we risk preserving the past instead of participating in what God wants to do next.

3. Dust thickens when we avoid the hard conversations.

In the name of peace, we stay silent about dysfunction. In the name of kindness, we ignore what is slowly breaking down trust, morale, and unity.

4. Dust accumulates when comfort becomes our highest goal.

The call of Jesus is not to ease but to obedience. When we prioritize our preferences over our purpose, we unknowingly trade life for maintenance.

5. Dust deepens when we fear the cost of change.

Change always comes with a price—loss, misunderstanding, resistance. But the cost of avoiding change may be far greater: stagnation, irrelevance, or slow decline dressed in politeness.

Not all dust is organizational. Some of it is deeply **personal**. Some are **emotional**—the residue of old wounds that were never truly healed. Some are **relational**—conflicts that were never named, just buried beneath Sunday smiles. Some are **spiritual**—where reverence becomes routine, and apathy quietly hides beneath polished language and proper behavior.

Here's the real danger: the longer the dust remains, the more it blends in. It settles not just on the pews and banners, but on our hearts. Over time, it begins to feel normal— familiar, like part of the furniture. Even holy. We forget what fresh air feels like. We often forget that movement is an integral part of the church's life.

Dust is not proof of death. But it is a sign of stillness. And stillness, left unchallenged, can become decay. So, we ask again, not in shame but in invitation: Where has the dust settled in your church? Where has it settled in your soul? Because the moment we notice it is the moment we can begin to invite the wind again.

Five Areas Dust Settles in the Church

Just as dust settles slowly and quietly in a home left undisturbed, it can accumulate in a church when movement ceases. When habits go unexamined, assumptions go unchallenged, and spiritual vitality is replaced by routine. Here are five areas where dust most often settles, and questions that can help stir the air again.

1. Mission Clarity

Many churches continue with long-standing programs and ministries without revisiting their original purpose. What may have once been a Spirit-led initiative becomes a sacred tradition simply because it's familiar. Over time, "We've always done it this way" is no longer a logistical explanation—it becomes a theological justification, even when the mission has been lost.

The result: Resources are drained. Volunteers grow weary. And the original passion fades beneath layers of good intentions that are no longer bearing fruit.

Dust-clearing question: "Why are we doing that which no longer serves the mission Christ gave us?" This question is not about tearing everything down—it's about realigning every ministry to the Great Commission and the Great Commandment.

2. Leadership Roles

In many churches, leadership positions are held out of loyalty, not calling. People serve year after year, not because they're passionate or spiritually equipped, but because no one else has stepped up—or they feel obligated. These roles become placeholders rather than launching pads.

The result: Vision stagnates. Ministries plateau. And gifted people in the congregation may stay disengaged because leadership is seen as fixed, rather than Spirit-led and dynamic.

Dust-clearing question: "Are our leaders called, equipped, and active in their roles—or just occupying them?" Healthy leadership invites new voices, prioritizes spiritual maturity over popularity, and refuses to let comfort dictate the structure of the church.

3. Worship Rhythm

Worship, when untended, can slowly become mechanical. Songs are sung, prayers are prayed, but hearts may not be lifted. The goal of encountering the glory of God is replaced by the goal of "getting through the service." Excellence becomes performance. Tradition becomes routine. Congregants become spectators.

The result: The wonder of worship fades. Services feel safe but hollow. Awe is replaced by apathy.

Dust-clearing question: *"Do our services lead people into awe and engagement—or merely familiarity?"* Vibrant worship doesn't always mean loud music or polished performance—it means intentional focus on the presence, worthiness, and beauty of God.

4. Evangelistic Passion

In too many churches, evangelism becomes a distant memory. The expectation that lost people will be saved is replaced with the hope that someone might eventually visit. Outreach becomes an event, not a lifestyle. Invitations are extended to church events, but not to Christ Himself.

The result: The church turns inward. Mission becomes maintenance. Baptisms become rare. And the joy of new birth in Christ is forgotten.

Dust-clearing question: *"When was the last time someone in our church personally shared the Gospel?"* Evangelistic passion is not a program—it's a culture. And culture changes when leaders model it, celebrate it, and pray for it.

5. Prayer Life

Prayer is the lifeblood of a church, yet it's often treated as background noise. In many congregations, prayer is often reduced to polite transitions between music and sermons, or to lists read aloud with little expectation. Instead of being a place of desperate intercession, the church becomes a place of religious routine.

The result: Power is replaced by routine predictability. Dependence on the Spirit is replaced by dependence on planning. And breakthrough is rarely sought—or expected.

Dust-clearing question: *"What would it look like if we became a church that prays?"* Not just a church *with* prayer, but a church *of* prayer. Where prayer meetings are full, spontaneous prayer is welcomed, and decisions are made on bended knee.

These five areas are not checkboxes—they are invitations. When we begin to recognize where dust has settled, we don't need to panic. We need to pray. We don't need to condemn—we need to cry out. The Spirit of God is still willing to breathe new life into old bones, but we must be honest about where stillness has replaced movement.

Dust is not the end. But it is a sign—a sign it's time to invite the Wind to blow again.

Jesus Didn't Avoid the Dust, He Died for It

Jesus didn't ignore the dust. He didn't walk around it or pretend it wasn't there. He entered it.

He came into a world layered with the dust of sin, sorrow, and death—a creation that had once been declared "very good" now groaning under the weight of brokenness.

He touched lepers. He knelt in the dirt to defend the guilty. He walked the dusty roads of forgotten towns and spoke life into forgotten hearts. But His mission didn't stop with compassion. It led Him all the way to the cross.

At Calvary, Jesus bore the full weight of humanity's dust—not just on His feet, but on His shoulders. The dust of pride. The dust of rebellion. The dust of dead religion. The dust of every wounded heart, every wayward church, every weary soul.

He didn't die for a polished version of us. He died for the real us—dusty, broken, and deeply in need of redemption.

And when He rose again, He didn't just wipe away the dust. He **breathed again**—the risen Lord, exhaling life into a world that had forgotten how to breathe. His resurrection wasn't just a moment of triumph; it was a moment of new creation. A signal that dusty hearts and dusty churches could come alive again.

That's why, when Jesus speaks to the churches in Revelation 2 and 3, His words are not harsh condemnations. They are fierce, holy love. He doesn't throw stones—He offers surgery. He doesn't say, *"You're too far gone."* He says, *"I stand at the door and knock."* He calls out compromise, not to embarrass, but to awaken.

He exposes apathy, not to shame, but to revive. He names what's wrong because He sees what can still be made right.

Love always tells the truth.

Jesus doesn't hide from the dust. He goes straight into it—and calls us out of it. So, if you feel the dust settling in your heart, your home, or your church, hear this: You are not beyond renewal. The One who formed us from the dust is the same One who redeems us through the blood. He is still breathing life. And He still delights to raise the dead.

A Church Story: The "Confessional" Church

The "Bethel" Church sits in a small community known as *Hell Hole Swamp*. By the time I was called as their young pastor at age 20, this 95-year-old congregation had dwindled to fewer than a dozen members.

Just three months in, I preached a series of messages titled *"The Dust We Ignore."* Each week, we examined areas where dust had quietly accumulated in the life of the church. The sermons were Scripture-soaked, gentle, yet courageous. For the first time in years, the members gathered to pray earnestly over the concerns we named together, as I was told.

The results were unmistakable: tears, truth, repentance, salvations, and growth. One elderly member said, *"I've been in this church since I was a child, and this is the first time we've admitted out loud that something's not right. And I think God is smiling at us for it."*

Within six months, The "Confessional" Church celebrated five baptisms, renewed prayer gatherings, and even launched a community partnership with a sister church.

Their story reminds us that renewal begins when a congregation is willing to name what is broken, return to the Gospel, and pray for God to breathe life into His church again.

Reflection Questions

1. Where has the dust quietly settled in your life and your church's life and ministry?

_____

_____

2. What truths have been hard for you and your church to face?

_____

_____

3. What would it look like for you to repent personally and *together* as a congregation?

_____

_____

Closing Prayer

Jesus, You are the center of everything. Forgive us for the ways we've drifted. Breathe life into us again—not through our strength, but through Your finished work. Let the Gospel not only save us, but also sustain us. Amen.

Breath to the Bones

Chapter 4

The Fire Returns

Prayer Is the First Sign of Renewal

Key Text: Acts 1:14
"All these with one accord were devoting themselves to prayer..."

A Church Story: The "Fading Fire" Church

I sat quietly on a middle pew of The "Fading Fire" Church, a once-vibrant congregation in the Carolinas. The building was more than adequate, sunlight streaming through stained-glass windows onto polished pews that glowed with a beauty that belied the weight in the room.

The pastor led the service faithfully, opening in prayer, offering announcements, recalling decades of ministry highlights, and closing again in prayer. Yet this Sunday told a different story than the record attendances and joyful baptisms of earlier years. Only a handful of people were scattered across the sanctuary. Their greetings were kind, but their eyes told the truth: they were tired, discouraged, and unsure of the future.

There was no scandal. No heresy. No collapse of leadership. Just the slow, steady fading of a flame. The music was sincere but subdued. The sermon was faithful but met with blank stares. What remained mainly was the weight of memories.

As I sat remembering how vibrant this church once was, a question rose in my heart like a mournful whisper: *When did their "prayer meetings" stop being prayer meetings?*

Their story is a sobering reminder that decline rarely comes all at once—it comes quietly, when prayer fades, passion wanes, and a church forgets its first love. Renewal begins the moment God's people bend their knees again, seeking His Spirit to breathe fresh life into weary souls.

Prayer is the First Fire to Fade

We started down this path in the previous chapter, but let's go deeper now.

If you walked into a declining church and judged its health by activity alone, you might be misled. The calendar is full. The lights are still on. Committees gather. Bulletins are printed. Choirs rehearse. Potlucks are planned. A visitor might even assume things are going well—at least on the surface.

But if you look closely, one crucial evidence is often missing from the rhythm of this church's life…

An authentic, meaningful prayer meeting.

The story is too common for many. Once the lifeblood of the church, the midweek prayer gathering has become, in many places, an afterthought. What was once a furnace of faith has cooled to a flicker. The room, once filled with tears and holy desperation, now echoes with silence or strained formality. It's not that people stopped *believing* in prayer. It's that something happened along the way:

Disappointment crept in. Weariness took root.
Distraction took over. And the flame began to fade.

Prayer didn't vanish. It just became passive. It moved from desperate dependence to religious duty. From breathing to whispering. From central to optional.

And this is no small shift. When a church stops praying, the engine of spiritual power stalls, regardless of how gifted the leaders are, how polished the services feel, or how full the calendar remains.

No church—no matter how well-organized, how long-standing, or how admired—experiences lasting renewal without returning to its knees. This is the forgotten flame. Not forgotten in theory, but in practice. Not denied but neglected. Not extinguished but unattended.

THE GOOD NEWS IS this flame can still burn again. Because prayer is not a program—it's a posture. It's not a line item—it's a lifeline. And God has never stopped answering the cries of His people when they humble themselves, seek His face, and ask for fire from heaven once more.

"....if my people who are called by my name humble themselves, and pray and seek my face and turn from their wicked ways, then I will hear from heaven and will forgive their sin and heal their land."

2 Chronicles 7:14

The first fire to fade must become the first fire to be rekindled.

Why Prayer Fades in the Modern Church

In many struggling churches today, prayer hasn't disappeared altogether—it's just been downgraded. It survives, but only as a supporting role.

We pray to open meetings, to close services, to bless meals, or to read down the list of health concerns and procedural needs. There's nothing wrong with these kinds of prayers. In fact, Scripture calls us to intercede for the sick, to seek wisdom, and to bring everything before God. But what's often missing is the **fire**—that soul-deep longing for God's presence, His power, and His purposes. What once felt central now feels supplemental. What once carried weight now feels like a whisper.

So, the question must be asked: *Why does prayer fade in the modern church?*

1. Prayer Is Uncomfortable
Real prayer disrupts us. It demands vulnerability, humility, and honesty. We must admit we are not in control.

We must stop pretending to be strong and start confessing our need. That kind of posture doesn't fit well in a culture built on image, efficiency, and self-sufficiency. And so, instead of entering into the discomfort of true intercession, we settle for polite, predictable words.

2. Prayer Is Slow

Prayer rarely fits into our schedules. It requires waiting, listening, lingering. But we are people of action. We want things fast, measurable, and efficient. We're trained by culture to multitask, to optimize, to make the most of every minute. But God is not bound by our pace. He works in seasons, not seconds. And so, we often abandon prayer—not because we don't believe in it, but because it doesn't move at the speed we prefer.

3. Prayer Isn't Easily Controlled

You can't script revival. You can't manage the Holy Spirit. True prayer invites God to speak, to lead, and to rearrange things as He sees fit. That kind of surrender threatens our systems. It threatens our comfort zones. And for leaders and churches that value control, prayer feels dangerous—because it is. Prayer puts God back at the center. Prayer hands over the reins.

4. Prayer Doesn't Always Yield Immediate Results

We like success stories. We're drawn to quick wins and instant outcomes. But prayer, especially when it's deep and desperate, often calls us to persist without visible fruit. It shapes us over time. It tills the soil. It breaks hard ground. But in a results-driven culture, if something doesn't "work" fast, we move on. And so, we replace prayer with programs, persistence with planning, and waiting with doing.

In the Kingdom of God... **Prayer *is* the work of God!** It is the labor of the Spirit through surrendered people. It is the act of moving heaven and shaking earth. It is the fire that precedes the fruit. It is the place where vision is born, where hearts are broken, where strongholds are shattered, and where revival begins.

The early church understood this. So did every generation that has experienced renewal. If we want to see fire again in our churches, we must return to the forgotten flame. We must recover the sacred discomfort, the beautiful slowness, the holy unpredictability, and the long, unseen labor of prayer. Because when the church prays—not just formally, but fervently—things begin to move. And where prayer fades, so does the power.

The Pattern of Prayer in Scripture

Throughout Scripture, God has never required a majority to begin a movement. He just needs someone—*anyone*—willing to pray.

- **Daniel** prayed alone in Babylon, kneeling by his window with no audience and no approval.

- **Elijah** stood alone on Mount Carmel, calling down fire in the face of spiritual compromise.
- **Jesus** regularly slipped away from the crowds—even from His own disciples—to pray in lonely places.
- **The early Church** didn't begin with thousands. It began with 120 souls in an upper room, waiting—not for results, but for the Spirit.

None of them had the crowd behind them. But **they had God with them.**

Before Peter preached...Before Pentecost ignited the world... Before the Spirit descended like fire... Before the Church exploded into existence and history was forever changed...

"All these with one accord were devoting themselves in prayer..." Acts 1:14

That is where it started. Not with a sermon, but with a *stillness*. Not with a stage, but with a *seeking*. The early Church was not birthed out of strategy sessions or mission statements. **She was born in a prayer meeting.**

The first believers had no buildings. No budgets. No platforms. No denominational structures. No seminaries. No seasoned church-growth consultants. What they had was a **promise**—that the Holy Spirit would come in power—and they had a deep, unified hunger to seek Him together.

So, they waited. They gathered. They humbled themselves. And they *prayed.* They didn't know exactly what was coming. They didn't know when. But they knew *Who* they were waiting for. And that was enough.

The upper room was not a place of performance—it was a place of preparation. Before there was power, there was posture. Before there was preaching, there was kneeling. And that pattern should never be forgotten because we live in a time when the Church often reverses the order. We plan first. We preach first. We act first. And if there's time—or crisis—we might pray.

But the early Church teaches us something timeless: The strength of our ministry is directly tied to the depth of our prayer. The fruitfulness of the local church is rooted in its faithfulness to wait on God.

The Spirit moves most powerfully through hearts that are emptied of self and full of expectation. And when the day of Pentecost came—on *God's* timing, not theirs—it wasn't a man-made revival. It was holy fire falling on a prayer-soaked people. From that fire, the Church burst into the world. Thousands believed. Communities were transformed. And the Gospel spread like wildfire. It all began in prayer. And it still does.

If we want to see a fresh move of God in our generation—if we long to see churches renewed, prodigals restored, and the spiritually dead brought to life—it will not come from programs or personalities. It will come the same way it always has:

From a people who refuse to move without the Spirit. From leaders who stop trying to manufacture what only God can ignite. From congregations that gather not just to *do church*, but to *seek heaven*.

The early Church didn't treat prayer as the warm-up—it was the war room. They didn't view prayer as a formality—it was their foundation. And through them, God shook the world. He still can. And He still will—if we return to the upper room.

Prayer and Renewal

There is an undeniable connection between prayer and spiritual breath (renewal). Just as our bodies cannot survive without breathing, neither can you nor the local Church thrive without praying. Prayer is not merely a spiritual discipline—it is the inhale and exhale of a local church that is alive to the presence of God. When prayer fades, the atmosphere grows still. But when prayer returns, so does breath. The Spirit begins to move—not because we've mastered a method, but because we've made space for His wind to blow again.

Where there is prayer, there is breath. Where there is breath, there is life. And, where there is life, there is renewal.

In Ezekiel 37, God brings the prophet into a valley of dry bones. It's a haunting scene—scattered remains of a people once alive, now silent, lifeless, and forgotten. As Ezekiel prophesies, something remarkable begins to happen: the bones come together, sinews form, flesh appears. The structure is restored. But they are still dead. The form is there, but the life is not—until the breath comes.

> "...Come from the four winds, O breath, and breathe on these slain, that they may live." Ezekiel 37:9b

And when the breath of God—*ruach*, the Spirit, enters them, they rise, not as spectators or survivors, but as a vast, living army.

The local church today often finds itself in a similar condition. The programs are in place. The people are present. The committees are functioning. The services are scheduled. The bones are together. But the question remains—are we truly alive?

In Acts 2, the early believers were gathered together. They weren't strategizing, entertaining, or marketing. They were praying. And suddenly, a sound came from heaven like a mighty, rushing wind. The house was filled. Hearts were set ablaze. Tongues were loosed. And the Church began to breathe.

The word for "Spirit" in both Hebrew (*ruach*) and Greek (*pneuma*) carries the same meaning—breath, or wind. Prayer is the act of opening the lungs of the Church to receive that breath once again.

Without prayer, there is no breath. Without breath, there is no life. And without life, there is no witness. No revival. No movement. No power.

But when we pray, the breath returns. And when the breath returns, the local church lives again.

The way forward is not complicated—but it is costly. It will cost time, comfort, and pride. But what we receive in return is priceless: the breath of God in our midst again.

The way forward begins with *repentance*. Before building any prayer strategy or launching new initiatives, we must first break the silence of our own hearts. Repenting of prayerlessness isn't just a leadership correction—it's a spiritual awakening. Often, a lack of prayer reveals where we've grown comfortable relying on our own strength rather than the Spirit of God. It's where control has crept in and quietly replaced dependence. This is where we must ask the hard questions: When did we stop praying with hunger? What has quietly taken prayer's place in our gatherings? Have we become more focused on outcomes than on the presence of God? We cannot rush this step. Repentance is not a detour on the path to revival—it is the road itself. It's the spark that can reignite the flame we forgot we had.

From there, don't worry about gathering a crowd: *Gather the few*. Revival rarely begins with the masses—it almost always begins with a remnant. Jesus didn't promise His presence to the multitudes, but to the two or three gathered in His name. Begin with just a handful who are truly hungry for God. Don't wait for critical mass. Just start. Establish a simple rhythm. Light a candle. Read a Psalm.

Kneel together. Let the Holy Spirit guide you. It doesn't need to be polished or programmed—just faithful. Just real. Just prayer.

As you gather, *pray with specificity*. Pray with Scripture. Vague prayers often reflect vague faith, but when we pray the Word of God, we align our hearts with His will. Our confidence grows. We don't have to fumble for words— God has already given us language for revival. Instead of merely asking God to bless our church, pray the words He's already given us. Ask Him to send out workers into His harvest. Plead for Him to revive us again, so that we may rejoice in Him. Ask for boldness to proclaim His Word and for hearts filled with spiritual wisdom and understanding. These aren't just good ideas. They are His promises—and He delights to answer the prayers He Himself inspired.

A revived church is a church whose heart breaks for the lost. When we pray for the lost, let's pray for them by name. True revival stirs evangelistic intercession. Begin with just five names—people in your life who don't yet know Christ. Write their names down. Pray for them each week. Encourage others in your church to do the same. As you call out their names before God, your heart softens, and your mission sharpens. And when someone on that list comes to Christ, the fire spreads. The church remembers why she exists.

Finally, *prayer must be taught through experience*, not just explanation. It isn't mastered in theory—it's caught in the presence of those who yearn for the heart of God. Let the next generation hear the groans of seasoned saints. Let children witness adults kneeling in surrender. Let new believers sit in a room where the Spirit stirs hearts through prayer. Don't hide your hunger. Let them see it. Let them feel it. When the church prays like God is really listening, others begin to believe that He is.

Prayer is the inhale and exhale of a living church. And if you want your church to breathe again—this is where it starts.

Signs of a Praying Church

How do you know when prayer has truly returned to a church? It's not about how many people attend a Wednesday night gathering. It's not about launching a prayer ministry or adding another time slot to the service schedule. Real prayer revival doesn't begin with programming—it begins with presence. And when God's presence is sought with hunger and humility, the signs are unmistakable.

1. You begin to see *spontaneity in worship.*

Prayer becomes a natural overflow into every moment, not confined to a slot on the schedule. It might rise up between songs, in the middle of a sermon, or as a quiet prompting for someone to kneel. There's a freedom in the room—a willingness to respond to the Spirit. Structure still exists, but it now serves the Spirit instead of restricting Him. Prayer becomes the oxygen of the gathering, not just a bridge between other moments, but the breath that fills them.

You also begin to see *confession and repentance*. When people truly encounter God through prayer, they stop pretending. Masks fall off, walls come down, and hearts soften. People confess—not because they're confronted publicly, but because the Spirit has quietly called them in. Repentance isn't seen as weakness but as worship. A spirit of humility begins to shape the culture. Rather than hiding sin, people bring it into the light because they believe grace will meet them there.

2. There are tears, and there are *testimonies*.

When God begins to move through prayer, both joy and brokenness are present. The atmosphere becomes tender. Tears flow—not just from pain, but from healing. Testimonies begin to surface—stories of answered prayers, restored marriages, healed memories, and surrendered lives. A sense of awe fills the room. It's not fabricated emotion, but real, holy vulnerability. People weep for the lost. They rejoice in redemption. They weep again over the beauty of grace. A praying church doesn't suppress emotion—it honors it as a sign of God's nearness.

3. People begin to linger.

In churches saturated by prayer, the service doesn't end because the clock says so. No one wants to leave. A holy stillness rests over the people. The altar fills with those who simply want more of Him. People remain—not from obligation, but because they are breathing something real. Leaders stop watching the clock and start watching the cloud. When the Spirit hasn't finished, the church waits. In a praying church, the benediction doesn't mark the end—it marks the sending.

4. Salvations become a visible fruit.

When a church is filled with prayer, people come to faith. The Spirit honors the cries of His people by drawing the lost to Himself. Visitors may not understand what they're feeling, but their defenses drop. The message strikes the heart. Baptisms become a celebration of new life, not a routine.

5. Evangelism becomes a joy, not a job.

In a praying church, evangelism is not seen as a task but as a blessing. Sharing the Gospel flows naturally out of time spent with the Lord. The more God's people pray, the more their hearts are filled with love for Christ and compassion for others. Evangelism becomes less about effort and more about overflow.

Members begin joyfully praying by name for friends, neighbors, and coworkers, trusting that God hears and answers. Those prayers open doors for meaningful conversations, and God faithfully draws people to Himself. Each answered prayer becomes a testimony of His goodness, fueling even more prayer and even greater boldness.

The result is not just growth in numbers, but growth through *new life*. New believers are welcomed into the family of faith, and the church rejoices. Evangelism is no longer a task to complete, but a joy to celebrate.

6. And then, there is *unity*.

In prayerless churches, tension tends to rise. Opinions clash, egos flare, and petty debates sap energy. But in praying churches, something different happens. People stop talking about each other and start talking to God—together. As they pray more, they compete less. Division yields to intercession. Disagreements soften under shared submission to the Spirit. Unity isn't forced—it's forged through surrender. It's hard to stay divided from someone you've wept beside in prayer.

The Significance of a Small Prayer Group

These signs aren't the result of hype. They're the fruit of a people who are desperate for God—not just to fix things, but to **fill them**. When prayer is restored to its rightful place in the church, everything else begins to align. Programs gain purpose. Preaching carries power. People become hungry. And the Spirit breathes again. You won't need to announce that revival has begun. The signs will say it for you.

Not everyone will immediately see the significance of an effective prayer life. Therefore, don't wait for everyone to want it. Start with a small prayer group. Revival rarely starts with a crowd. It usually begins with a remnant. If you're longing to see a deeper culture of prayer in your church, know this: **not everyone will be ready.** Some will resist. Some will misunderstand. Some will dismiss it as emotional, unnecessary, or even uncomfortable.

Some believers may say, *"We already pray,"* meaning they open meetings with a few moments of routine words. Some may say, *"This feels too intense,"* as if passion for God's presence is a disruption rather than a desire. And that may not be okay with you, so start praying with those who want to experience a more significant prayer life. God doesn't wait for consensus to move. He responds to hunger.

You decide to seek a more meaningful prayer life, knowing that true, faithful prayer is rarely popular at first. *Why?* Because…It calls us out of comfort. It asks us to slow down. It invites us to wait on God rather than rush ahead with our own plans. But faithful prayer—persistent, hidden, humble, Spirit-dependent prayer—**is how the fire starts.**

Don't wait for perfect alignment before you seek the face of God. Don't wait for a committee to approve a move of the Spirit. Don't wait for everyone to be equally passionate before you kneel in the sanctuary, gather in a classroom, or sit in stillness before the Lord. Start with and join the few. Start with and join the willing. Start with yourself.

The breath that God desires to breathe into the bones is still available. But we must open our mouths. We must open our lungs. We must return to prayer. Because no matter how good our planning, programming, or preaching may be, without prayer, the church holds its breath. And the world doesn't need a breathless church. It needs a church that breathes again.

A Church Story: The "Praying" Church

The "Praying" Church, located in a small rural community, was averaging less than thirty in attendance and facing an uncertain future. The sanctuary echoed with memories, but vitality was fading. Concern was growing, yet the people chose one path forward—not a new program, not a rebrand, not a dynamic pastor. They chose prayer.

Wednesday prayer meetings became true prayer meetings. While some people prayed publicly, others prayed quietly. Some wept. Some confessed. On Sundays, I would arrive early to pray over empty pews before anyone else entered. Together, the congregation called out to God, asking Him to send His breath again. At first, nothing seemed to change. But then…unchurched people began to visit. A middle-aged woman gave her heart to Jesus and was baptized. Attendance began to grow. Over 100 people gathered for a Homecoming Service. Slowly, former members returned, and within six months the congregation was averaging 50 in worship—not because of strategy or marketing, but because people prayed and God answered.

This was not revival by human design, but resurrection by divine mercy. The "Praying" Church had lost its breath, but by prayer, the Spirit of God caused the church to breathe again.

Their story reminds us that prayer is not preparation for renewal—it is the very place where renewal begins.

Reflection Questions

1. What role does prayer currently play in your life and the life of your church?

_____

_____

2. What would it take for you and your church to prioritize prayer again?

_____

_____

3. Who could you invite to begin a new journey of prayer with you?

_____

_____

Closing Prayer

Lord, return us to our knees. Let our hunger be holy. Let our prayers be bold. Forgive us for replacing Your presence with plans. Rekindle the flame of prayer until our church breathes again with heaven's wind. Let this house be called a house of prayer once more. Amen.

The Fire Returns

Chapter 5

The Altar Rebuilt

When Leaders Renew, Churches Renew

Key Text: 1 Kings 18:30
"Then Elijah said to all the people, 'Come near to me.' And all the people came near to him. And he repaired the altar of the Lord that had been thrown down."

A Church Story: The "Altar Kept" Church

The "Altar Kept" Church, a fast-growing evangelical congregation, embraced a fresh, effective approach to the altar call. At the close of each service, the pastor warmly invites anyone sensing God's leading to come forward.

In addition to receiving inquirers up front, he invites them to a Hospitality Room where friends and leaders are ready to listen, pray, and walk with them through decisions of faith. These moments create opportunities for both formal and informal conversations about Scripture and prayer and their significance when making decisions.

The "Altar Kept" Church reminds us that renewal is not only found in strategy, but in a posture of humility—when leaders and members together demonstrate their trust in God to move in hearts and awaken lives through the Gospel.

A Broken Altar and a Silent Church

Before fire fell from heaven… before the crowd cried out, "The Lord, He is God!" … before revival swept through a weary nation… Elijah rebuilt the altar.

It had been neglected for too long. Stones lay scattered. Worship had been replaced by performance. Conviction had crumbled under compromise. The people of God were torn—caught between the false promises of Baal and the fading memory of the One who had delivered them. And the altar—the place where they once met with God—was in ruins.

It's easy to read 1 Kings 18 as ancient history. But look around. It's not just a story from the past—it's a mirror for the modern Church. Leadership fatigue is high. Moral failures have become tragically familiar. Pastors are burning out—or quietly walking away. Congregations are skeptical and scattered. Vision is blurry. Conviction is rare. And prayer is often an afterthought.

We are a church culture longing for fire, but too many altars lie in pieces. We want the results of revival without the rebuilding that revival requires. But fire does not fall on convenience. It falls on consecration.

Before God answers by fire, He calls His people to rebuild what has been broken. And it starts with leaders— not polished, platformed personalities, but humble servants willing to repent, to rebuild, and to return to the altar of prayer, purity, and holy surrender.

The altar is not a stage. It's not a strategy. It's a place of sacrifice. A place of death. A place of fire. If we want to see God move again, we must stop admiring the ruins and start picking up the stones.

This is the invitation: Rebuild the altar—one prayer, one act of repentance, one surrendered life at a time.

IN SCRIPTURE, the altar is never just a passive structure—it is always a place of divine encounter and human response.

Wherever you see an altar, you see a moment where heaven touches earth. It's not about the stones themselves; it's about what happens on them. The altar is the center of surrender, the platform of repentance, and the starting point of revival.

From Genesis to Revelation, altars mark the moments where God and His people meet in the most powerful ways. For Abraham, it was the place of trust and obedience. For Elijah, it was the place where fire fell. For the early church, it was the Spirit-filled gathering of surrendered hearts. The altar has always been the space where God's presence is felt and His power revealed.

At the altar, sin is confessed—not glossed over, not excused, but brought honestly before God with the hope of grace. Sacrifices were laid down—yes, physical ones in the Old Testament, but always symbolizing something deeper: the surrender of hearts, wills, futures. The altar was never about ritual alone. It was about a relationship.

It was at the altar that the fire of God would often fall—not on distracted crowds, but on consecrated spaces. God's power descended not on programs or performances, but on places of preparation. The altar was where the covenant was renewed—where God reminded His people of who He is and who they are. It was where promises were reaffirmed, and hope was restored.

Again and again, the altar was where leaders were restored. God didn't meet them at the podium, but at the place of brokenness and surrender. He called Moses from the burning bush. He met Isaiah in the temple. He restored Peter by the fire after failure. The altar is where God does His deepest work in His people—especially in His leaders.

In every generation, God calls His people back to the altar—not just to remember, but to respond. Not just to observe, but to offer. Because it is still true today: the altar is where revival begins.

WHEN THE ALTAR IS BROKEN, it's never just a logistical issue—it's a spiritual alarm. A crumbling altar reveals more than just forgotten stones; it reveals forgotten surrender. It tells the story of a church that may still be gathering but no longer meeting with God in power. The structure might stand, but something essential has gone missing.

A broken altar means worship has lost its weight. Songs may still be sung, but the wonder is gone. Reverence fades. The presence of God becomes a concept, not a reality. The room fills, but the heart doesn't tremble.

It means the people have forgotten how to weep. Tears that once flowed in repentance and awe are replaced with safe prayers and shallow emotion. The ache for holiness is dulled. The hunger for revival is dismissed. And the soul of the congregation grows quiet—too quiet.

It means leadership has grown polished but prayerless. Sermons are delivered, schedules are managed, and strategies are crafted—but all without kneeling. The fire of private devotion dims under the spotlight of public performance. The pulpit speaks, but heaven doesn't seem to move.

It means the gatherings continue, but the glory has departed. The room may buzz with energy, but it lacks presence. The Spirit no longer stirs freely because the altar has been left in disrepair. And when that happens, God's voice begins to feel distant—not because He has moved, but because we have.

When the altar is neglected, worship becomes an empty ritual. Leadership becomes a stage act. The people become scattered in focus and unity. And the spiritual temperature grows cold—cool enough to be comfortable, but far too cold to ignite anything.

In that environment, we settle. We keep moving, but we're not going anywhere. We confuse activity for anointing and mistake production for presence. But beneath it all, something inside us knows: it's time to return to the altar. Because only at the altar does the fire fall. Only at the altar does the breath of God return.

Rebuilding the Altar Today

Rebuilding the altar in our time is not about reviving old traditions or replicating ancient rituals. It's not about the construction of a platform or the renovation of a sanctuary. It is about recovering a spiritual posture that has been lost. It is about returning to the heart of worship—where God is not simply acknowledged but adored. Where His presence is not just welcomed, but essential.

To rebuild the altar is to reclaim the fear of the Lord, where worship is no longer approached casually, but with trembling wonder. It means gathering not for performance or preference, but to encounter the holiness of God. It is to remember that the One we sing to is also the One before whom angels cover their faces.

It means restoring the authority of God's Word—not as a helpful resource, but as the voice of the living God. In a rebuilt altar culture, truth is not adjusted to fit our preferences—it is received with reverence and obeyed with joy. Scripture becomes the compass again, not just a decoration for the walls or a footnote to our opinions.

It also requires the renewal of leadership humility—where pastors, staff, and members alike kneel before God before they ever presume to speak for Him. Rebuilding the altar demands that we lead from our knees, not just from our pulpits. It's not about personality-driven platforms—it's about Spirit-led surrender.

A rebuilt altar becomes a declaration. It says, "We will not move without You." It whispers, "We would rather be still in Your presence than busy without Your power." And it cries, "We surrender everything again—not for show, but for fire."

Revival fire never falls on altars we admire. It falls on altars we rebuild—stone by stone, prayer by prayer, tear by tear. And when it does, the church breathes again.

When Leaders Renew, Churches Renew

No church renewal is from the pews alone. While every member plays a role in the life of the body, true renewal doesn't begin with crowds—it begins with leadership. It doesn't start in strategy sessions or committee votes. Attendance campaigns or calendar adjustments do not spark it. Church renewal begins in the hearts of the leaders.

In 1 Kings 18, Elijah doesn't begin by confronting the crowd or launching a national movement. He doesn't gather focus groups or form a planning team. Instead, he calls the people near and begins to repair the altar that had been left in ruins. Before there was fire from heaven, before there was national repentance, one leader was rebuilding what others had neglected.

That scene is more than historical—it's deeply instructional. Because the altar wasn't just about national worship, it was about spiritual leadership. The broken altar mirrored the fractured state of spiritual authority in the land. And until that altar was restored, no fire could fall.

Elijah models what every pastor, elder, deacon, and ministry leader must embrace: *you cannot lead a church*

back to life if you're unwilling to return to the altar yourself.
Personal repentance always precedes public renewal.
Leadership renewal is not optional—it is foundational.

If the altar of prayer, dependence, and humility has been ignored in the leader's life, then the church may stay busy, but it will not burn with holy fire. The Spirit moves most powerfully through surrendered vessels. That's why church renewal begins when leaders stop performing and start returning to the quiet place, to the surrendered place, to the sacred place where God speaks and leaders are remade.

Before we ask God to move among the people, we must let Him move in us. Before we plead for fresh vision, we must kneel in fresh repentance. Leadership renewal is not just the first step of church renewal—it's the most essential one.

The first calling of any pastor, elder, deacon, or ministry leader is not to fix the church. It is to rebuild the altar of their own soul. Before revival can sweep through a congregation, it must first find a resting place in the heart of its leaders. Programs won't spark it. Passionate sermons won't sustain it. Renewal begins in secret—where leaders bow low again, not to perform, but to surrender.

The truth is, many of us are trying to lead while bleeding. We keep moving forward, week after week, even as something deep inside feels fractured. We stand before people with vision in our mouths, but wounds in our hearts. The altar beneath us—our place of communion with God—is often cracked or neglected. And yet, we keep pressing on, hoping ministry momentum will cover the emptiness we haven't faced.

Too many of us are carrying bones we've never fully named.

There's the quiet grip of unconfessed sin—habits or patterns we've hidden, thinking we can manage them privately while leading publicly. There's the slow creep of cynicism—the erosion of trust in people, in the process, and sometimes, if we're honest, even in God. There's the fear of man—the exhausting urge to please everyone, to avoid conflict, to measure our worth by approval. There's the bitterness left behind from past wounds—betrayals that haven't healed, burnout that's gone unacknowledged, conflict that left a scar. And then there's the exhaustion—masked as endurance—where our souls are running on fumes, but we keep showing up, because the calendar doesn't pause and the needs don't stop.

But here's the hard truth we can't ignore: *the church cannot rise if its leaders have no breath left in them.* A suffocating leader cannot lead a breathing church. If we truly long for God to move *through* us again, we must let Him move *in* us again. This renewal starts by returning—not to the spotlight, but to the secret place, not to the next plan, but to the altar. Not to exert more effort, but to surrender more deeply.

This is where renewal begins—not with fixing the church, but with letting God renew you.

Signs the Leadership Altar Is Broken

The signs of a broken leadership altar are not always loud or dramatic. They may not come with headlines or public scandal. Instead, they often appear quietly—subtle cracks in the soul, small compromises in integrity, or a gradual cooling of passion for Christ. Yet, though quiet, these signs are telling. They reveal that something vital has shifted, that the fire on the altar has begun to fade. So, what are the signs?

1. Vision Fades into Routine

One sign is when vision fades into routine. Leadership gatherings that once carried weight, expectation, and a sense of God's leading slowly become dominated by calendar logistics and maintenance updates. The boldness of faith is replaced with the safety of familiarity. We begin to manage rather than minister. There's no longer a sense of spiritual anticipation—only task lists. When this happens, it's more than a leadership slump—it's a cracked altar. Because vision is more than strategy; it is spiritual fire. And where there is no vision, not only do people drift, but leaders do, too.

2. Trust Begins to Erode

Another sign is when trust begins to erode and is replaced by turf. Ministries become silos. Communication gets guarded. Leaders start protecting their "area" rather than advancing a shared mission. Collaboration suffers. Suspicion creeps in. This kind of division isn't just a relational issue—it's a spiritual one. Turf wars in leadership are often fueled by fear, insecurity, or pride. But where there is humility and prayer, trust can be rebuilt. A divided leadership team cannot shepherd a unified church. The altar must be repaired.

3. Absence of Prayer

A third sign is the absence of prayer among leaders. When leadership meetings begin without intercession— when plans are discussed more than God is sought—it's a sure indicator that something vital has been lost. Leaders cannot effectively guide God's people without first listening to Him. Planning without praying might produce activity, but it won't produce anointing. A leadership team that prays together breathes together. Without the breath of God, no amount of planning can revive the body.

4. Sin Goes Unconfronted

A fourth sign of a broken leadership altar is when sin goes unconfronted. Gossip, immorality, laziness, or pride are sometimes tolerated in leadership under the banner of "keeping the peace" or "not rocking the boat." But peace that comes at the cost of truth is not peace at all—it is quiet decay. If sin is allowed to linger, unchecked and unaddressed, the altar is not only broken—it's dishonored. God cannot bless what leaders refuse to confess and confront. Restoration can happen, but only after truth is told.

5. Character is Undervalued

Finally, the broken altar shows itself when character is undervalued. In too many churches, gifting is elevated above integrity. Charisma overshadows humility. Popularity or tenure become qualifications, while spiritual maturity is overlooked. But the altar of leadership is not built on talent—it's built on trustworthiness, holiness, and surrender. Churches that elevate giftedness over godliness may rise quickly, but they crumble just as fast. Revival doesn't fall on performance. It falls on purity.

Such moments are not to be ignored. They serve as gracious warnings—signals from God that it is time to return. Return to the place of surrender, where leaders once yielded their whole selves to Him. Return to the place of prayer, where dependence on God was the source of every strength. Return to the place of purity, where holiness mattered more than success.

Leaders, This is Your Moment!

Leader, this is your moment—not to manage systems, maintain appearances, or push through with more hustle. This is your moment to return. Not to return to how things used to be, but to return to the altar. Not to lead from charisma or capacity, but to lead from brokenness, surrender, and holy dependence.

"But I say, walk by the Spirit, and you will not gratify the desires of the flesh." Galatians 5:16

God is not asking you to revive your church with your own strength. He's not placing the weight of renewal on your shoulders as if it depends on you. He's inviting you to rebuild the altar—not a physical one, but a spiritual one. An altar of prayer. An altar of repentance. An altar of trembling reverence where leadership no longer performs but bows low before the King.

You don't need to manufacture revival. You don't need to manipulate outcomes. You don't have to pretend to be strong when you're tired. You simply have to return to the place where fire falls—on surrender.

Throughout Scripture, God never sends fire on empty ground. He sends fire on prepared altars—on the places where His people have said, "We're not moving without You. We won't fake it. We won't force it. We need You."

And when leaders rebuild the altar—when they pray like it matters, weep like it's personal, confess like it's urgent, and wait like He's near—the fire does come. Holy fire. Purifying fire. Not the fire of hype or noise, but the fire of heaven. It falls on hidden hearts before it ever fills public spaces.

And when that happens—when leaders go first, when the altar is no longer neglected—the church will follow.

Not because of pressure, but because of presence. The people of God recognize when something real is burning. They know when heaven has touched earth again.

So, leader, don't lose heart. Don't settle for a ministry of motion without power. Rebuild the altar. One prayer. One act of repentance. One moment of surrender at a time. And trust—when the altar is restored, the fire will fall.

A Church Story: The "Faithful" Church

The "Faithful" Church, located in a town and country community, faced a spiritual crisis. Recognizing the urgency of the moment, one of the deacons reached out to their local Baptist association for guidance. Through a series of prayerful meetings, the deacons, alongside their interim pastor, came to realize their greater need: not merely to solve a problem, but to seek the heart of God for their future.

Together, they opened the Scriptures. They prayed with humility. They repented where repentance was needed. And slowly but unmistakably, the church began to breathe again. Worship was renewed with joy and sincerity. Lost people began attending. Community outreach was relaunched. Giving increased. Attendance grew. None of this was the product of a program or plan—it began at the altar, when leaders surrendered themselves to God.

What followed was not a manufactured turnaround but a genuine move of God. The "Faithful" Church discovered new life because her leaders first chose to bow at the altar, and God met them there.

Reflection Questions

1. What parts of your leadership altar have fallen into despair?

_____

_____

2. Where have you substituted competency for intimacy with God?

_____

_____

3. Is there a relationship on your leadership team that needs healing?

_____

_____

Closing Prayer

Lord, forgive us for leading without listening. For planning without praying. For building without bowing. We return now to the altar—to the place where You meet us, purify us, and commission us again. Heal our leadership teams. Restore our credibility. Give us the courage to lead with a vision that honors You, not just pleases people. And send fire again—not for our glory, but for Yours. Amen.

The Altar Rebuilt

Chapter 6

A New Fellowship
Where the Gospel Shapes Every Relationship

Key Text: Acts 2:42, 47b
"And they devoted themselves to the apostles' teaching and the fellowship, to the breaking of bread and the prayers ... And the Lord added to their number day by day those who were being saved."

A Church Story: The "New Fellowship" Church

The "New Fellowship" Church, a young congregation in the metro area, tried one effort after another to regain health. On paper, they had what many church planters consider essential—young families, a young pastor, contemporary worship, and sound theology. However, the constant relocation from one rented space to another took a toll on both the leaders and the people.

In their weariness, the pastor reached out to the local Baptist association and asked if they could temporarily meet in the association's facilities "before we give up." The answer was yes.

For the first time in a long while, the congregation no longer had to set up and tear down each week. Freed from that burden, they refocused on Biblical priorities—building Gospel-centered relationships and cultivating true biblical community. Finally, they could breathe again—literally and spiritually.

As they devoted themselves to the apostles' teaching, life began to flow back into the church. Within months, The "New Fellowhip" Church experienced a renewed fellowship, and today they are thriving in their own permanent facility as the Lord continues adding to their number those who are being saved.

From a Skeleton to a Body

The valley was filled with bones. Dry. Disconnected. Forgotten. What once was a people had become a scattered, lifeless remnant. And then God spoke.

As Ezekiel obeyed and prophesied, something astonishing happened:

"So I prophesied as I was commanded. And as I prophesied, there was a sound, and behold, a rattling, and the bones came together, bone to its bone." (Ezekiel 37:7)

Sinews formed. Flesh covered them. Structure reappeared where there had only been ruin. But even then, they weren't alive. Not yet.

"And I looked, and behold, there were sinews on them, and flesh had come upon them, and skin had covered them. But there was no breath in them." (Ezekiel 37:8)

This moment—the reassembling of what was scattered—is not just poetic or symbolic, it is profoundly **theological**, deeply **missional**, and urgently **practical**. Because the Church is not just a group of individual believers. The Church is a **body**—connected, interdependent, Spirit-filled, and called to move *together*.

> *And the first step toward life in the valley wasn't breath. It was **alignment.***

Too many churches function more like **spiritual skeletons** than **spiritual bodies**—fragmented, loosely connected, technically present, but functionally paralyzed. Committees meet, but hearts don't connect. Programs run, but relationships are shallow. Attendance happens, but unity is absent.

Renewal is not just about getting people in the building. It's about reuniting hearts in the presence of God. It's about the scattered becoming whole again. It's about moving from survival to spiritual **structure**—where each part is joined to the other in love, humility, and purpose.

> *Church health begins with reconnection.*

Not just in attendance, but in affection. Not just in ministry titles, but in mutual dependence. Not just in proximity, but in partnership. This kind of reassembly isn't something we can manufacture. It is something only the **Holy Spirit** can create.

*When the bones come together—when the scattered become the body—**renewal is near.***

The Gospel Shapes Every Relationship

In Acts 2, the early church didn't explode with life because of strategic planning, impressive buildings, or a professional clergy. What marked them was something far deeper— something undeniably supernatural: a devoted fellowship. They broke bread together. They worshiped side by side. They gave generously, even sacrificially. They endured suffering with joy. They prayed and studied the Word with unwavering commitment. And what was the result?

"The Lord added to their number daily those who were being saved." Acts 2:47

Why did that happen? Because the watching world saw something they couldn't find anywhere else—real, authentic, Christ-shaped community. It wasn't just compelling doctrine that drew them in—it was the witness of shared life. The Gospel didn't just sound true; it looked beautiful.

Unfortunately, in many churches today, we've quietly traded devoted fellowship for surface-level friendliness. We shake hands, but we rarely share burdens. We sit together on Sundays but suffer alone the rest of the week. We exchange pleasantries, but not confessions. We know each other's names, but not each other's stories. And the result is that many congregations remain polite—but powerless.

The Gospel doesn't just reconcile us to God; it reconciles us to one another. It doesn't just form individuals—it forms a family. It doesn't just fill a building—it builds a body. When a church reclaims this kind of Gospel-shaped, Spirit-born community, something happens. The bones don't just come together—they begin to move. Life returns. Breath fills the lungs again. And the Church stops merely attending... and starts becoming.

What a Gospel-Shaped Community Looks Like

Churches often say they value "community," but what that word means can vary wildly. In many congregations, "community" has been reduced to little more than calendar events or designated rooms in a building. We schedule a potluck, set up chairs in the fellowship hall, share a few laughs after service, and call it community. But a Biblical Gospel-shaped community is something far deeper. It's not a vibe. It's not an event. It's a way of life.

Biblical Gospel-shaped community is not defined by casual proximity or shared routines. It is marked by deep,

Spirit-formed relationships where grace, truth, and love are lived out in real time. It's not simply gathering around food every few months—though meals can be sacred. It's not polite conversation over coffee in the lobby or keeping up with each other in a Facebook group. And it certainly isn't a fellowship hall that no longer hosts any real fellowship. Community isn't a place—it's a practice. It's not something you visit. It's something you build.

True community looks like this: relationships rooted not in hobbies or politics or personality types, but in a shared identity in Jesus Christ. It looks like people sacrificing their time, energy, and comfort to meet one another's needs. It's spiritual conversations that go deeper than small talk. It's asking hard questions, bearing one another's burdens, and praying through the struggles—not just posting prayer hands online. It's welcoming outsiders not as guests, but as long-lost family members. It's confronting conflict with truth and grace and choosing forgiveness when it would be easier to walk away. It's noticing when someone is weary—holding space for the hurting and speaking life when someone has forgotten their worth. It's the body of Christ acting like a body.

This kind of community isn't convenient—it's costly. But it's also one of the clearest signs that a church isn't just surviving—it's breathing. When a congregation embraces biblical Gospel-shaped community, it becomes a place where life is shared, faith is deepened, and the presence of God is felt through His people. It's more than fellowship. Its formation. It's not just a program. It's a pulse.

Why Churches Lose Biblical Fellowship

If biblical fellowship is so vital to the health of the local church, why do so many congregations quietly lose it?

The early church described in Acts 2 was marked by vibrant, Spirit-filled fellowship—characterized by shared meals, mutual care, sacrificial generosity, and spiritual unity.

But in many churches today, what remains is little more than surface-level friendliness. Smiles are exchanged, hands are shaken, and greetings are offered—but the depth, transparency, and transformative fellowship described in the New Testament are noticeably absent.

What happened? How does something so essential become so rare?

Consider the following five reasons:

1. Wounded Relationships

One of the most common reasons is wounded relationships. Few things fracture fellowship more quickly than unresolved conflict. The lingering effects of past church splits, gossip, leadership betrayals, or moral failures often go unhealed. People may return to the building, but not to true community. Trust is broken. Hearts retreat behind polite smiles and guarded conversations. Members may continue to serve, but they no longer share. A culture of distance replaces a culture of discipleship. Without intentional healing, churches become collections of individuals— physically present but emotionally absent. Forgiveness, reconciliation, and honest lament are not optional—they are essential to rebuilding trust and restoring true fellowship.

2. Overprogramming

Another culprit is overprogramming. In many churches, the schedule is bursting with events and activities, yet the soul of the church remains dry. Ministry calendars are full, but a meaningful connection is missing. Church members are busy attending, volunteering, organizing—but rarely truly connecting. Busyness can mimic vitality while masking spiritual isolation. The more drained people become by church activity, the less energy and margin they have for authentic relationships. Over time, people confuse doing church with being the church. Sometimes, simplicity—not more structure—is the path back to shared life.

3. Generational Gaps

Generational gaps also weaken the fabric of fellowship. When older and younger believers live in parallel but separate lanes—failing to learn from, listen to, or value one another—division quietly forms. The church becomes segmented by age rather than united by identity in Christ. Older members may feel dismissed or irrelevant; younger members may feel unheard or underutilized. Yet each generation has God-given gifts meant to enrich the other. When we ignore or minimize those gifts, we impoverish the whole body. True fellowship across generations doesn't happen accidentally—it must be cultivated through humility, intentional conversation, and mutual honor.

4. Cultural Individualism

Cultural individualism has also crept into the church. Modern life trains us to prioritize autonomy, efficiency, and control. We build private lives, curate our online presence, and filter our interactions. But the way of Jesus is profoundly different. Biblical fellowship is inconvenient, messy, and sacrificial. It demands that we slow down, open up, and walk with others in their joys and sorrows. Many believers today love Jesus but resist the vulnerability of His body. They want faith without friction. But until we confront the idol of individualism, we will never fully experience the joy and transformation that come through Gospel-shaped community.

5, Transparency Feels Unsafe

Finally, many churches have unknowingly cultivated environments where transparency feels unsafe. Grace may be preached from the pulpit, but if it's not practiced in the pews, people will hide. When confession is rare and appearances are rewarded, vulnerability becomes risky. So believers wear masks. They bury their struggles. They edit their stories to fit the room. But real fellowship cannot survive in a culture of performance. It requires honesty. It requires people to show up with their doubts, their sin, their scars—and find not shame, but love. Where grace is lived, not just taught, people begin to breathe again.

When local churches discover or rediscover biblical Gospel-centered community, true fellowship happens, and they become places where the Gospel is not just heard—it's embodied. Wounds are healed. Generations walk together. Burdens are shared. Lives are transformed. Because where the Spirit breathes, the bones don't just come together—they come alive.

The challenges that have eroded fellowship in the local church are real—but they are not permanent. God is still giving breath to the bones. Jesus is still building His Church. The Holy Spirit is still binding hearts together across wounds, generations, personalities, and preferences. The bones can come together again, but only when we stop settling for surface-level connection and begin to pursue the kind of Gospel-shaped community described in Scripture.

How to Re-build Gospel-Shaped Community

True fellowship and Gospel-shaped community don't happen by accident. It must be cultivated. In a culture marked by isolation, speed, and self-sufficiency, community must also be reclaimed.

The early church didn't just attend services together— they belonged to one another. Their bond wasn't built on convenience or shared interests, but on their shared identity in Christ.

The Holy Spirit created a family out of strangers, a people out of individuals, a church out of saved sinners.

118

The following are ways to build or re-build a Gospel-shaped Community in your church:

1. Teaching

Today's churches can begin to build or rebuild that same kind of community. It begins with teaching. Many believers have never been taught what it means to be the body of Christ—not as a metaphor, but as a living, breathing, interdependent reality. Scripture gives us this vision clearly. In 1 Corinthians 12, Paul writes that we are one body with many members, and every part matters. In Romans 12, we are called to love sincerely, to rejoice and weep together, and to honor one another. In Ephesians 4, Paul says the body grows strong as each part works in love. When churches reduce community to event attendance, they weaken it. But when they embrace their identity as the body of Christ, community begins to deepen.

2. Small Groups

The path forward does not begin with massive programs or a perfectly designed small group structure. It begins small. It begins with one table, one shared meal, one honest conversation. The real work of fellowship starts in living rooms, over coffee tables, in moments of vulnerability. People want to be invited to know and to be known. Where hospitality leads, healing tends to follow. Never underestimate the spiritual power of a simple meal shared in Jesus' name.

3. Real Stories

Community also requires space for real stories. Testimony builds trust. People don't connect to one another through abstract theology alone—they connect through honest stories, shared struggle, and tangible grace. Churches that prioritize space for storytelling—through testimony nights, open prayer times, or vulnerable leadership—begin to tear down walls. When one person confesses pain, doubt, or need, others begin to exhale and say, "I can relate to that." In that moment, community is born.

4. Generational Connection

Generational connection is another vital element. A healthy church isn't just multigenerational on paper—she is multigenerational in practice. Older and younger believers need one another. When energy and wisdom walk side by side, the Spirit moves in profound ways. But this doesn't happen automatically. Churches must design intentional ways for generations to share life: mentoring relationships, intergenerational small groups, or prayer partnerships. The result is a church where no one is too old to matter or too young to be heard.

5. Equipped to Handle Conflict

Along the way, the church must also be equipped to handle conflict. Real fellowship doesn't avoid tension; it grows through it. Conflict is not the enemy of community—unresolved conflict is.

Churches must teach how to speak the truth in love, how to follow the path of reconciliation laid out in Matthew 18, and how to extend grace even when it's hard.

Leaders should model this. Small group facilitators should be trained in it. And the whole church should learn that forgiveness is not weakness—it's maturity. The more a church learns to forgive, the more it learns to flourish.

6. Celebrate the Wins

Finally, we must celebrate the wins of community. What gets celebrated gets repeated. When someone in grief is surrounded by their small group, share that story. When meals are delivered, prayers offered, or needs met in quiet faithfulness—acknowledge it. Let the body see the beauty of itself in motion. Public celebration reinforces private formation. It reminds people what's possible. It creates a culture where Gospel-shaped community is not only expected but desired.

Rebuilding community is not quick work. It takes time, intention, and prayer. But it is worth every step. Because when the Spirit forms true fellowship, the church becomes more than a gathering. It becomes a family. And when the world sees that family—marked by grace, truth, and love— they will long to come home.

Using the Meal Table as a Tool for Renewal

Throughout church history, some of the most sacred and Spirit-filled movements didn't begin in sanctuaries or stadiums. They began around tables—ordinary meals made holy by the presence of God and the vulnerability of His people.

In Acts 2, the early church broke bread in their homes and ate together with glad and sincere hearts. It wasn't just a meal—it was a means of grace, a rhythm of shared life that embodied the Gospel. Jesus restored Peter not in a synagogue, but at breakfast—on a beach, by a charcoal fire, with four tender words: "Do you love me?" The Last Supper wasn't a sermon or a program. It was a table, set with bread and wine, where Jesus redefined how His followers would remember Him forever.

Even now, across the globe, in house churches and persecuted communities, tables remain the sacred center—where Scripture is opened, food is passed, burdens are shared, and lives are quietly transformed.

Why the table?

Something holy happens when people slow down, open their homes, and share more than just food. The rush of performance is replaced by presence. Walls begin to crumble. Hearts soften. The Gospel moves from theory to touch, from proclamation to participation. Revival doesn't always need a stage. Sometimes, it needs a dining room.

If your church building feels empty, start with your table.

Don't wait for the next program or sermon series to invite someone. Open your door. Set an extra plate. Begin with what is simple, sacred, and slow. Invite someone new, someone who's lonely, or someone who's been quietly slipping in and out of the church for years. Let the meal breathe. There's no need to rush. Silence is welcome. So is laughter.

Ask the kind of questions that open hearts: "How's your soul?" "What are you learning from God?" "Where are you feeling stuck or stirred?" Let joy fill the room. Laughter is holy too—it's often the sound of people feeling safe enough to be real.

And above all, make the Gospel visible through your welcome. Hospitality is not about entertaining—it's about incarnating the love of Christ. When you listen well, when you show care without agenda, when you create space for people to be seen and heard, you are offering them a glimpse of grace.

Here's a truth: a hundred sermons won't do what one shared meal can. Renewal isn't always loud. Sometimes, it simmers in the kitchen. Sometimes, it begins with a fork, a question, and a quiet prayer. And often, it's at the table where the Spirit begins to move again.

A Church Story: The "Table" Church

The "Table" Church, located in a growing suburb of a major metropolitan city was a new church plant. I had the privilege of serving as the church planter. It was an exciting work—many came to faith in Christ, followed Him in baptism, and the church grew primarily through new converts.

Rapid growth came with the challenge of building close relationships among so many newcomers. Some of the church's leaders began noticing the gap and simply responded by inviting others to share meals with them and their families after church or during the week. There was no agenda—just food, honest conversation, lots of laughs, and space for relationships to grow.

Quickly, the spirit of the church began to change. Friendships formed. Prayer requests increased. People showed deeper care for one another. What began as fellowship meals became the heartbeat of the Gospel community. While increased attendance was not the primary goal, the congregation continued to grow.

Within five years, average worship attendance reached the seventies and eighties. Eighty-seven people joined by profession of faith and baptism, and seventeen more by transfer from sister churches. What began as a mission plant became a vibrant family of faith—reminding us that Gospel-centered fellowship is rooted in Gospel-shaped relationships.

Reflection Questions

1. What does fellowship currently look like in your church? (shallow, structured, deep, fragmented?)

_____

_____

2. Where has isolation crept in—either relationally or generationally?

_____

_____

3. How can your church move from friendliness to family?

_____

_____

Closing Prayer

Lord, thank You for placing us in a body, not in isolation. Forgive us for treating community as optional. Rekindle real love among us. Help us weep with those who weep and rejoice with those who rejoice. Restore trust, unity, and grace in our fellowship. And let our togetherness display the beauty of Christ to a watching world. Amen.

A New Fellowship

Chapter 7

The Church Breathes
Welcoming the Spirit Back into the Church

Key Text: Ezekiel 37:9–10

"Then He said to me, 'Prophesy to the breath; prophesy, son of man, and say to the breath, Thus says the Lord God: Come from the four winds, O breath, and breathe on these slain, that they may live.' So I prophesied as He commanded me, and the breath came into them, and they lived and stood on their feet, an exceedingly great army."

A Church Story: The "Breath-LESS" Church

In a rural community in the Carolinas, The "Breath-LESS" Church had grown weary from years of conflict. What had once been a sweet fellowship was now marked by conversations that began with, "He said. She said. They said." The joy of their life together was being drained away.

When the leadership asked me to meet with them, everyone arrived prepared. The pastor had notes in hand. The clerk brought detailed minutes, recording every motion and word. Leaders came with carefully rehearsed speeches. Yet for every account of what had happened, there was another version—each colored by perspective and emotion. The congregation was anxious. The leaders were perplexed. And the atmosphere grew heavier with each exchange.

Finally, I stopped the discussion. "Let's pray," I said, "and ask the Holy Spirit what He wants to do in this meeting tonight. Let's let Him know that we want Him here, and we want to hear His voice."

In that moment, papers were set aside. Pens were laid down. Heads bowed. And the weight of human words gave way to a holy silence, as the congregation made room for the only One who could bring peace, unity, and renewal.

The Forgotten Member of the Trinity

In some churches, the Holy Spirit has become the forgotten presence in the room. We preach the love of the Father. We exalt the sacrifice of the Son. But when it comes to the Spirit, we often grow silent—or, at best, cautious.

Pastor and author Francis Chan captured this tension in his book *Forgotten God*[4], where he lamented how the Church has functionally sidelined the very One Jesus promised would be our power, our guide, and our breath. And he's right. In practice, some believers treat the Trinity as Father, Son, and Holy Bible—substituting doctrine for the living presence of the Spirit.

The neglect of the Holy Spirit in many local churches is rarely intentional, but it's often rooted in subtle fears or past experiences. Some have seen spiritual expressions taken to unhealthy extremes—manipulated emotions, theatrical displays, or false promises—and, in response, have chosen to keep the Spirit at a safe distance. Others carry wounds from previous church experiences where "Spirit-filled" settings led to pride, division, or unbiblical teaching. Over time, this leads not to openness, but to guarded suspicion.

For many leaders, the deeper issue is control. The Spirit moves in ways we can't predict, doesn't follow a script, and rarely fits into a tidy order of service. While we may not say it aloud, we often prefer predictable outcomes over supernatural interruptions.

At times, theological misunderstanding plays a role. The Holy Spirit is treated as a vague force or optional doctrine rather than the fully Divine, fully present third Person of the Trinity—the very breath of God given to empower the Church.

And finally, in a church culture shaped by professionalism, excellence, and production, we've made more room for performance than for power. But the Spirit doesn't require polish—He responds to surrender.

What Jesus Said Still Stands

Before ascending into heaven, Jesus didn't leave His disciples with a conference strategy or a five-year ministry plan. He gave them a promise:

"You will receive power when the Holy Spirit has come upon you, and you will be My witnesses..." Acts 1:8

He didn't promise programs, applause, staff, structure, or certainty. He promised power. And apart from that power, we are unable to bear witness to the risen Christ in a way that transforms hearts or revives dead churches. Programs may impress. Sermons may inform. But only the Spirit can bring life.

Church renewal is not merely about getting the bones in place. It's about the breath—the very breath that hovered over the waters at creation in Genesis 1, that raised Jesus from the dead in Romans 8, and that filled the Upper Room at Pentecost in Acts 2. The Holy Spirit is not a theological footnote. He is the flame that ignites, the wind that moves, the breath that gives life, the power that transforms, the guide who leads, the comforter who sustains, the purifier who refines, and the reviver who awakens. Until we remember and rely on Him, we will continue to have churches with structure but no Spirit, motion without movement, and sound without substance.

Characteristics of Spirit-Dependent Church

In a Spirit-dependent church, prayer is no longer a formality or just a transition tool. It becomes the first instinct, not the last resort. People pray with expectation, believing that God will move in real time. Intercession is welcome. Space is made—not just for words, but for the presence and power of the Spirit to act.

The following are characteristics of a Spirit-dependent church:

1. Leadership Marked by Humility

Leadership in a Spirit-dependent church is marked by humility. It's no longer about preserving control, but about seeking what God is doing and joining Him. Pastors and teams ask, "What is God saying in this moment?" Decisions flow from discernment, not dominance.

2. Worship Becomes Responsive

Worship becomes responsive. It shifts from performance to presence. People stop spectating and begin participating. Hands lift, tears flow, silence settles, and joy breaks out—not because of a setlist, but because the Spirit is actively stirring hearts. There's freedom to follow where God leads.

3. Preaching Changes

Preaching also changes. It becomes more than a well-rehearsed delivery. It becomes an encounter. The preacher is not only well-prepared, but also Spirit-sent. The Word is proclaimed with fire and conviction—not just to inform, but to awaken, convict, and call people to respond.

Spirit-dependent churches make room for more than programs —they make room for transformation. They leave space for confession, for healing, for quiet reflection and bold response. They don't rush past conviction or ignore the nudge of the Spirit. The altar becomes a place not just of decision, but of encounter.

And at the heart of it all is trust in the Spirit's timing. They don't try to force outcomes or manipulate growth. They know that some breakthroughs take time. They rest in God's pace. They move when He says move and wait when He says wait—because they believe the Spirit knows how to build the Church better than we ever could.

At the heart of Spirit-dependence is a radical shift in how we ask questions. Instead of: "What do we want to do?" We begin to ask:

"Holy Spirit, what do You want to do here?"

And that one question—if honestly asked—can change the course of a meeting, a sermon, a worship service... even a church's future. Because when the Church surrenders its strategies to the Spirit, we stop simply managing what we've built—and start participating in what God is breathing to life.

How the Holy Spirit Renews the Church

The Holy Spirit is not an accessory to church life. He is not optional, marginal, or secondary. He is the breath, the fire, the wind—the very presence of God among His people. Without the Spirit, the Church becomes a body without breath, a lamp without oil, a form without fire. But when the Holy Spirit is truly welcomed, He does far more than comfort—He renews.

The following are ways the Holy Spirit renews the local church:

1. He brings dead places back to life.

He renews dry bones into living members. He turns stagnant religion into a Spirit-empowered mission. Revival is not the result of strategy or structure—it is the work of the Spirit.

2. He Convicts

When the Holy Spirit is welcomed into the life of the Church, the first evidence is conviction. He reveals sin, not to shame us, but to restore us. As Jesus said, "When He comes, He will convict the world concerning sin and righteousness and judgment." (John 16:8) His conviction is never a harsh condemnation—it is a loving call to come home. People begin to confess what they once concealed. Worship becomes real. Hearts soften. Hidden things are brought into the light. Conviction is the beginning of awakening.

3. He Empowers the Hands

But the Spirit doesn't stop at awakening hearts—He empowers hands. As Paul writes in 1 Corinthians 12, the Spirit gives gifts to each believer for the good of the body. These aren't antiquated roles. They are tools for mission— prophecy, service, wisdom, teaching, discernment, healing, and more. The Spirit equips the Church not to be spectators but servants, not to be passive but passionate. A revived church is a gifted church—every part active, every gift aflame.

4. He Guides

He also guides. In a world saturated with information, the Church needs revelation. The Spirit leads with more than logic—He speaks through Scripture, confirms with peace, directs through burden, and unites through prayer. Jesus promised, "When the Spirit of truth comes, He will guide you into all the truth." (John 16:13) Spirit-filled churches do not ask, "What's popular?" They ask, "Where is the Spirit leading us now?"

5. He Unites

And where the Spirit leads, He unites. The Holy Spirit binds hearts together. As Paul exhorts in Ephesians 4, "Make every effort to keep the unity of the Spirit through the bond of peace." He tears down walls—between old and young, rich and poor, black and white, wounded and whole. He replaces gossip with grace, rivalry with trust, and suspicion with love. Division cannot stand where the Spirit reigns. Unity is one of His most visible signatures.

6. He Fills

Finally, the Spirit fills. He does not merely visit—He takes up residence. When He is honored, He satisfies the deepest hunger in the church: not for more programs, but for more of God. His filling brings courage where there was fear, strength where there was weakness, purity where there was compromise, and worship that overflows from awe. This is not emotional hype. This is the holy presence of God, making His people alive again.

True renewal is not a formula. It is a fresh filling. It is not a plan. He is a Person. When the Holy Spirit is welcomed, honored, and obeyed, the Church doesn't just function—she breathes. And where the Spirit breathes, dead bones rise.

A Church Story: The "Freedom" Church

For more than a century, The "Freedom" Church had been faithful to the Gospel. Yet, like some congregations, she had become stuck in tradition. Routine shaped their gatherings. Attendance was plateaued, at best. Fellowship centered on food and orderliness became the goal.

The church had called many pastors over the years, but this time, something was different about their "new" pastor. In a short amount of time, everything changed. With strong pastoral care and a passionate evangelistic heart, he convinced the people of his genuine love for them and their families—and his deep concern for their eternal destiny. God used his ministry to stir something new within the congregation.

Worship grew deeper and more reverent. Preaching became transformative. Attendance and membership increased. People were coming to faith in Christ, following Him in baptism, and inviting unchurched friends and neighbors. The fruit of their faith was evident to the community around them.

The story of The "Freedom" Church reminds us that when God raises a Spirit-led shepherd, the Holy Spirit can free a congregation from routine and breathe new life into His people.

Signs the Spirit is Being Welcomed Again

When the Holy Spirit is no longer sidelined but truly honored, sought, and obeyed, the atmosphere of a church begins to shift. This shift isn't always sudden or loud—but it is unmistakable. It doesn't come from strategy or personality. It comes from surrender. These signs don't point to human success. They point to holy presence. They mark a church that is not just operating—but breathing.

1. Freedom in Worship

One of the first signs is freedom in worship. It's not chaotic or hyped—it's holy. The Spirit brings a freedom where people are no longer trying to impress or perform. Instead, they respond to the presence of God. Songs feel less like routine and more like a reverent offering. People sing with tenderness, raise their hands with reverence, and weep or rejoice without fear of judgment. Silence becomes sacred. Lament and joy find space in the same room. Leaders stop relying on scripts and start leaning into the Spirit. God is no longer just talked about—He is encountered.

2. Deeper Conviction in Preaching

Another sign is a deeper conviction in preaching. The pulpit becomes more than a platform—it becomes a place of piercing and awakening. Sermons are no longer simply informative. They are transformative. Listeners don't just take notes. They take inventory. God's Word begins to stir affections, confront sin, and awaken hearts to His presence. It's not the cleverness of the preacher that moves people— it's the weight of the Spirit working through the Word. The voice behind the sermon may be familiar—but the conviction is unmistakably Divine.

3. Repentance

Then comes genuine repentance. Not surface-level apologies. Not polished confessions. Real repentance. People stop managing their image and begin mourning their sin. They stop posing and start kneeling. The altar, once a forgotten piece of furniture, becomes a sacred space again. Not because of emotionalism, but because grace is drawing people home. Leaders go first. Members follow. Relationships once fractured begin to mend. Confession becomes normal. Repentance becomes expected. And healing begins—not from shame, but from mercy.

4. Participation in Ministry Widens

As this happens, participation in ministry widens. The Church stops functioning like a staff-led institution and begins to look like a Spirit-activated body. People recognize that ministry isn't for a few professionals—it's for every believer. Spiritual gifts begin to surface. A retired teacher disciples a teenager. A young adult leads intercessory prayer. A once-quiet church member speaks life into someone else, and chains fall. Leaders stop hoarding ministry and begin equipping the saints for it. The question is no longer "Who's in charge?" but "Who's being faithful with what God has entrusted to them?"

5. Fruit

And when all this is happening, something else begins to unfold—fruit that no one can explain. People get saved—sometimes the very ones the church had nearly given up on. Broken friendships are restored. Families reconciled. A spirit of generosity begins to spread—without a capital campaign. Forgiveness flows. People begin hearing the call of God—into missions, into foster care, into church planting, into neighborhood ministry. And it becomes clear: this is not the result of human planning. This is the result of divine power. The Spirit is not merely moving behind the scenes. He is bearing fruit in plain sight. And no one can take credit—because it's unmistakably God-breathed.

When the Holy Spirit is welcomed again, churches don't just come alive—they begin to thrive in ways only heaven can explain.

"...they lived and stood on their feet, an exceedingly great army."—Ezekiel 37:10b

A Church Story: The "Hopeful" Church

Stepping out in faith and trusting God with the outcome is never easy. Often, the right decision is clear, but the timing feels uncertain. Concerned about the future of his congregation, the pastor of The "Hopeful" Church reached out to me for guidance. After prayerful conversations with him and his leadership, they agreed to begin a renewal process.

As the process unfolded, the leadership team came close to making an important decision about being replanted by a sister church. Then, unexpectedly, there was a pastoral change. For many, it was confusing. Yet after regrouping, the church prayed and chose a different path, clinging to hope and trusting in the Lord's timing.

In God's providence, the pastor of The "Hopeful" Church retired, and the church called a new pastor to lead them forward. He is thriving, and so is the church. Today, they have every reason to be hopeful about their future— because God's timing and plans are always perfect.

Characteristics of Welcoming the Holy Spirit

Churches that truly thrive are not sustained by programs, personalities, or even traditions, but by the presence and power of the Holy Spirit. When God's Spirit is welcomed, He brings life to weary souls, breathes fresh fire into worship, and awakens the church to her mission. Renewal is never manufactured—it is received. And it is received in churches that make room for Him.

The following are common characteristics of churches that welcome the Holy Spirit. These marks are not formulas to follow but fruits that flow from a posture of humility and surrender. They remind us that when the Spirit is given freedom to lead, the church becomes more than an organization—she becomes a living body, breathing with the life of God.

1. They experience transformation.

This is what happens when the Holy Spirit fills the Church. It's not just about improvement—it's about transformation. It's not just excitement—it's awakening. It's not about programs that work—but people who burn with Holy fire.

2. Dead hearts come alive.

Dead hearts come alive. What sin once hardened, the Spirit softens. People who used to sit unmoved under the preaching of the Word begin to weep in worship, confess in humility, and sing with sincerity. The Spirit awakens the soul to the beauty of Christ again. What was once mere religion becomes a relationship. What felt like duty becomes delight. The cold becomes fire. The spiritually dead don't simply behave better—they come to life.

3. Tired leaders find new courage.

Tired leaders find new courage. Pastors and ministry leaders, once weighed down by pressure and fatigue, suddenly remember why they said "yes" in the first place. The burdens of ministry remain, but the wind beneath them shifts. Vision replaces cynicism. Joy begins to push out exhaustion. The Spirit revives not just the congregation, but the shepherds too.

4. Scattered people find unity.

Scattered people find unity. Where division once reigned, peace begins to flow. Where preferences and politics once created walls, now prayer and purpose hold people together. Age, background, and culture matter less than Christ. A Spirit-filled church becomes a Spirit-formed family—one body, moving together in peace. As Ephesians 4:3 reminds us, we are to "make every effort to keep the unity of the Spirit through the bond of peace."

5. Ordinary Christians begin walking in power.

Ordinary saints begin walking in power. One of the most evident signs that the Spirit is at work is when ordinary people start doing extraordinary things. The stay-at-home mom intercedes like a warrior. A teenager launches a Bible study in their school. A retiree shares the Gospel with boldness in the grocery store. Gifts begin to stir. Callings come alive. Ministry breaks out beyond the platform— because the Spirit is on the move.

6. The church's mission advances.

And the mission of the church begins to advance in ways no human effort could engineer. Fruit appears—fruit that no strategy planned, no budget funded, and no committee controlled. People are saved. Marriages are restored. Addictions are broken.

7. Reconciliation happens.

Reconciliation happens. People with low incomes are served. The Gospel moves beyond the church walls, not because of what the church is doing for God, but because of what God is doing through His Church. As Zechariah 4:6 declares: "Not by might, not by power, but by My Spirit, says the Lord."

This is what revival looks like when the breath of God fills the Church. Not hype, but holy movement. Not just bodies in the pews—but life in the bones.

A Church Story: The "Spirit-Filled" Church

The "Spirit-Filled" Church, located in a growing rural area, is a mid-sized church that had begun to plateau. The people were faithful, the teaching was clear, and the attendance was steady—but there was little fruit. Their beloved pastor shared that while the programs were sound and the systems were well-run, he had depended more on sermons and structure than on the Holy Spirit. However, everything shifted after a meaningful spiritual encounter with the Holy Spirit while on a mission trip to Russia.

He returned to the pulpit changed—humbled, awakened, and hungry for more of God. Those close to him, me included, sensed it immediately. He shared, "The Holy Spirit spoke to me." He began setting aside time devoted solely to prayer, worship, and listening for the voice of God. He invited others to join him. The pastor started preaching through the Scripture with fresh eyes, emphasizing the power and presence of the Holy Spirit. He also began equipping his leaders to identify and walk in their spiritual gifts. Over time, spontaneous prayer times became normal, not forced.

What followed wasn't flashy—but it was unmistakably real. People responded at the end of sermons with confessions. A grieving family who was walking through a loss shared how they felt carried and covered by their church like never before. There were no headlines, no dramatic campaigns. But the church began to breathe again—not because of a better strategy, but because the Spirit had breathed life into the pastor and into the people, again.

Reflection Questions

1. How would you describe your church's current relationship with the Holy Spirit—neglected, cautious, or dependent?

_____

_____

2. What teachings or practices might be unintentionally minimizing the Spirit's role?

_____

_____

3. Where have you relied on human wisdom instead of Divine power?

_____

_____

Closing Prayer

Holy Spirit, we need You. Forgive us for planning without praying, working without waiting, and leading without listening. We open our lives, our leadership, and our church to You. Fill us again. Breathe into what is dry. Empower us to live, love, and lead with courage. Fall fresh on us, and let the world see not our strength, but Your Spirit. Amen.

Chapter 8

The Sent Church

Back to the Streets. Back to the Mission.

Key Text: Matthew 28:19-20
"Go therefore and make disciples of all nations, baptizing them in the name of the Father and of the Son and of the Holy Spirit, teaching them to observe all that I have commanded you. And behold, I am with you always, to the end of the age."

A Church Story: The "Sent" Church

The "Sent" Church is in a growing city located within the metro area of a state capital. The occasion was the beginning of a full afternoon, set aside for a series of listening sessions at The "Sent" Church—a time for members to share both their church stories and their Jesus stories.

Around the table sat three couples, their faces marked with the blend of hope, weariness, and quiet curiosity that so often fills the room in moments like these.

In the back of the room, a young woman sat quietly as she listened to the older couples share. At the end of the session, with a few minutes to spare, the young lady slowly pulled her chair forward and began to share her story. Her voice was gentle, and her story was real. She shared how she had walked through deep hurt and pain—wounds that had left her searching for healing and hope. Then, with tears in her eyes, she described how she encountered Jesus, how the church had welcomed her, and how she had made her profession of faith.

As she spoke, the room fell still. Every person leaned in, captivated by the power of her testimony. We sat in awe, reminded that the Gospel is not an abstract truth but a living reality that changes lives.

When she finished, I looked around the room and asked, *"How many of you had ever heard her Jesus story before?"* One by one, heads shook. Not a single person raised a hand.

Then I turned to her and asked, *"Have you ever heard their stories—how they came to Christ and what He has done in their lives over the years?"* She smiled gently and said, *"No."*

In that moment, the silence spoke volumes. It was a holy realization: the Spirit was reminding us that our Jesus stories are not to be kept to ourselves. The "Sent" Church celebrates when God's people share their stories; they not only bear witness to His grace in ways that knit hearts together and strengthen the body of Christ, but those stories also need to be heard in the streets and communities where lostness lives.

The Church Rises for a Reason

God does not breathe life into dry bones so that they can lie there and feel better about themselves. As in Ezekiel's vision, when the bones assemble and the breath of God fills them, something astonishing happens:

"They lived and stood on their feet, an exceedingly great army." Ezekiel 37:10

They don't sit. They don't form a committee. They stand. Because when God revives His people, it's never for passivity. It's always for a purpose.

Why does God raise the Church? Not for comfort. Not to resume routines. Not to admire the miracle of revival like a trophy behind glass. He raises her to move. He raises her to march. He raises her to go to war—not with flesh and blood, but with the powers and strongholds that hold a dying world in chains.

This is the holy sequence of heaven: from death to life, from life to community, and from community to mission.

Renewal that doesn't move is just resuscitation. But when the Spirit truly fills a church, she does not return to business as usual—she rises with fire in her bones and a cry in her heart:

"Here we are, Lord. Send us."

Maintenance is not an option. Comfort is not the goal. We were not revived to sit—we were revived to stand. And when the Church stands, hell trembles.

Many churches experience a measure of renewal—just enough to feel alive again, but not enough to fulfill their calling. They rediscover prayer. They restore relationships. They repair broken leadership structures. Hope begins to rise. Worship deepens. The atmosphere shifts. But then... they stop.

They gather, but they don't go. They heal, but they don't help. They are renewed—but not sent.

This is not a full renewal. It's rehabilitation without release. Like a patient who regains strength in the hospital, only to remain in bed, never stepping back into the world they were meant to reenter.

A church that is renewed but not reengaged in mission is a church still in recovery. Restoration is not the finish line—it's the starting gate. True renewal always leads outward.

Jesus made this unmistakably clear. When He appeared to His disciples after the resurrection, He didn't merely comfort them. He *commissioned* them:

> *"As the Father has sent Me, so I am sending you."*
> John 20:21

This is not a suggestion or a strategic option. It is the very essence of renewal. The Father *sent* the Son. The Son *sends* the Church. Mission is not the reward of renewal. It is the reason for it.

Churches are not restored so they can simply enjoy better services, cleaner buildings, or smoother operations.

They are restored to join Christ in His redemptive mission—to seek and save the lost, to shine light in the darkness, and to bring hope to the broken. Anything less than that is not renewal. It's just rearranged furniture in a room no one has been invited into.

The test of true renewal is not just how alive a church feels—but how far that life flows into the streets, the neighborhoods, and the nations.

The Danger of the Inward Spiral

Decline rarely begins with bad theology or external opposition. It often begins with something much subtler: the slow spiral inward. When a church loses her outward focus, it doesn't usually happen with a decision—it occurs by drift. We stop asking kingdom questions and start asking comfort questions. Instead of *"What does our community need?"*, we ask, *"What do our people want?"* Instead of *"How can we reach the lost?"*, we ask, *"How can we keep everyone happy?"*

This is the path of least resistance—and it always leads downhill. The result? Spiritual claustrophobia. The church becomes smaller on the inside than it is on the outside. Rooms are filled, but hearts are empty. Ministries continue, but mission fades.

The Gospel becomes trapped inside the building—talked about, celebrated, even studied—but not shared. And yet, the Gospel was never meant to be contained. It was meant to be carried into living rooms and around lunch tables, into classrooms and city halls, into conversations and nations. The Good News does no good if it never leaves the room.

Jesus Didn't Say, "Come"—He Said, "Go"

The Great Commission is not an optional add-on to church life—it is church life. It's not a program. It's not an event. It's not a department. It's the DNA of a Spirit-filled people.

Jesus never said, "Go and grow your church." He didn't say, "Go and protect your comfort," or "Go and make your name great." He said,

"Go and make disciples of all nations"
(Matthew 28:19)

That is not just a command—it's a calling. It's our missional identity.

We are not a seated people. We are a sent people. Sent to our cities, where loneliness and poverty hide behind lovely lawns and busy schedules. Sent to our co-workers, who are searching for purpose in all the wrong places. Sent to our neighborhoods, where anxiety, addiction, and brokenness live behind closed doors. Sent to the hurting, the overlooked, and the forgotten. Sent to the nations, because God's heart has never stopped beating for the whole world.

To ignore that call is to wither slowly—even while the machinery of church activity keeps running. To obey that call is to come fully alive.

A church may survive without mission, but she will never thrive. And eventually, she will suffocate on her own inwardness. The local church was never meant to be a museum for the saints. She was called to be a movement for the lost.

The question isn't whether we will be sent. We already are. The question is: Are we still willing to go?

What is a Missional Church?

A missional church is more than a place where people gather on Sundays—it is a community of believers who see themselves as sent by God into the world. Instead of focusing only on programs or buildings, a missional church embraces her identity as a people on mission with Christ. Every member is called to live out the Gospel in everyday life—at home, at work, in the neighborhood, and beyond. In this way, the church doesn't just *do* missions; she *is* missional, joining God in His work of bringing hope, healing, and salvation to the world.

1. Every Member Embraces Being a Missionary

A missional church is a church where every member embraces their identity as a missionary. It's a people who live with purpose, rooted in the Gospel and sent into the world by the Spirit of God. In a missional church, mission is not something reserved for a few—it's the calling of all. Every gathering becomes preparation. Every sending is intentional. Every believer is commissioned.

2. They Love Their Community

They see their community as a field to be loved. The neighborhood isn't just the location of the church—it's the church's assignment. People aren't treated like projects; they're honored as image-bearers. And the church doesn't wait for them to come. She joyfully steps into their lives with compassion, humility, and hope.

3. They Live-Out the Gospel Intentionally

They live with Gospel intentionality every day. Evangelism isn't an awkward task to complete—it flows naturally. Believers share their stories, their meals, and their faith. Conversations are seasoned with grace. The Good News shows up in everyday places—homes, schools, workplaces, parks, and coffee shops—spoken not just with words, but with kindness and courage.

4. They Steward Their Buildings for Ministry

They steward their buildings as tools for ministry. Facilities are no longer trophies—they become launching pads for service and connection. From food pantries to prayer gatherings, from youth mentoring to neighborhood events, every square foot is leveraged for Kingdom impact.

5. They Equip and Release Their Members

They equip and release people for their unique mission fields. Members stop waiting to be invited into ministry—they're empowered to carry Christ into their everyday lives. Whether they work in boardrooms or classrooms, construction sites or kitchen tables, they see those places as sacred. They know they've been sent there.

6. They Build Authentic, Lasting Relationships

They build authentic, lasting relationships. Love becomes the strategy. Flash and performance fade. Missional churches value presence—real presence. They invest time and attention into deep friendships that open doors for Gospel conversations and mutual transformation.

A missional church is a community on the move—grounded in love, fueled by the Spirit, and focused on the harvest. They gather to worship, grow, and be refreshed. Then they go—sent with joy and filled with power. They don't wait for the world to come to them; they walk into the world with open hands and open hearts. Because for them, mission isn't just something the church does. It's who the church is.

A Church Story: The "Multiplying" Church

The "Multiplying" Church had a clear vision and the determination to pursue it: to reach their city for Christ. Their commitment was evident in the way they invested their resources to engage their community. They hosted the city's largest Vacation Bible School, drawing more than 1,000 children with events that included a 100-foot banana split and even a parachutist. On July 4th, they invited the community to the local high school for an evangelistic service that concluded with a $10,000 fireworks show.

But beyond the big events, their most ambitious strategy was to plant churches in every multi-housing community in the city—37 locations in all. On launch Sunday, The "Multiplying" Church sent out eight new church plants at once. I was part of that movement, planting a congregation at Basswood Manor Apartments with my wife and young son. Within ten months, our church had grown to 100 people and celebrated 17 baptisms. The other seven new plants also saw significant fruit.

Encouraged by these results, The "Multiplying" Church continued to pursue their vision of planting churches across the city—multiplying Gospel presence in places where it had not been before.

Steps Toward Becoming Missional Again

The Church was born on mission—sent by Jesus, filled with the Spirit, and called to carry the Gospel into every corner of the world. Becoming missional again isn't about going backward; it's about returning to our true identity. It's a joyful rediscovery of why we exist: to love our neighbors, share good news, and live as light in a dark world. When a church reclaims its mission, it doesn't shrink—it shines. The steps that follow are practical ways to reignite that flame and step confidently into the calling God has given us.

1. The Neighborhood Story

Every neighborhood holds a story—and a mission waiting to be embraced. Start by asking, "Who has God placed around us?" Look beyond your walls and reconnect with your community.

What are their hopes, dreams, and challenges? Listen with compassion. Walk your streets prayerfully. Meet community leaders. Pray over schools. Get to know the names and needs of local business owners. Rediscovering your neighborhood is a joyful step toward loving your city as God does—one relationship, one story, one open door at a time.

2. Sunday is a Beautiful Celebration

Sunday is a beautiful celebration—but it's also a launching point. Worship together with joy, and then send one another out with purpose. Let your preaching, discipleship, and ministries equip people to live the Gospel in everyday life—from Mondays in the classroom to Saturdays in the grocery store. When believers see every day as sacred and every place as a mission field, the church becomes an unstoppable force for good.

3. Evangelism Becomes Life-Giving

Evangelism becomes life-giving when it's shared by all. Every believer has a story worth telling, and every Gospel conversation is a moment worth celebrating. Equip your people with confidence, compassion, and clarity. Make questions like, "Who are you praying for?" and "Who are you inviting?" part of your church's joyful rhythm. When the whole church embraces the mission, evangelism becomes less about obligation and more about overflow.

The world needs the Gospel—and so does your neighborhood. God has already placed your church near schools, shelters, prisons, and neighborhoods that long for hope. Engage them not as problems to solve, but as people to love. Build bridges of compassion. Ask with expectancy: "If our church disappeared, how would our city feel the difference?" Let the answer be a resounding testimony of your love in action.

The goal isn't to gather more, but to send more. Empower your people to go with purpose—into homes, workplaces, campuses, and communities. Celebrate every step of obedience: the teacher who prays for students, the business leader who lives with integrity, the family who invites a neighbor to dinner. Support church plants, commission missionaries, and budget boldly for Kingdom expansion. A thriving church doesn't just grow in—it multiplies out.

Breaking the Barriers to Missional Renewal

Every church has the desire to make a difference—and the potential to do it. But sometimes, that potential gets buried under hesitation, past hurt, or simple busyness. The good news is that none of these barriers is permanent. With prayerful leadership and Spirit-led courage, they can be broken. What stands in the way today can become the very ground where renewal begins. God is not waiting for a perfect church—He's looking for a willing one. These common challenges can become launching points for a fresh move of mission and hope.

1. Change

Change can be unsettling—but it's often the first step toward renewal. When a church begins to live on mission, comfort zones are stretched, and routines are reexamined. That's not a threat—it's a sign of growth. Some will hesitate. Some may even push back. But that's okay. Be patient as a leader. Keep preaching courage. Keep modeling obedience. Let people see the joy and fruit that come from stepping out in faith. Transformation doesn't happen all at once—but it always begins with one bold "yes" to God.

2. Regrets

Many churches carry wounds or regrets from seasons of decline, division, or missed opportunities. But the Gospel is not just good news for individuals—it's good news for congregations. God delights in using broken vessels. In fact,

He specializes in it. Your past does not disqualify you—it prepares you. Let your story of redemption become your platform for mission. When God restores, He always does it for the sake of others.

3. Underestimate

Never underestimate what God can do through a faithful few. Throughout history, small churches have made a big difference—planting new congregations, launching ministries, transforming communities, and reaching people others overlooked. Your size is not your ceiling—it's your starting point. When even a handful of people say, "Here we are, Lord—send us," heaven takes notice. Mission is not about how many you have, but how surrendered you are.

4. Calendars

Church calendars can get crowded with good things that quietly edge out the best things. Mission doesn't require more activity—it requires more intentionality. Take time to evaluate: Are our ministries aligned with our mission? Are our events creating impact or just maintaining motion? Pruning isn't punishment—it's preparation. As you clarify your priorities around the Gospel, your church will move forward with greater focus, joy, and fruitfulness.

A Church Story: The "Missional" Church

The "Missional" Church, located in an established suburban community of a large metro area, is being led by their pastor to pursue an intentional strategy of living out Acts 1:8. Their mission is clear: to develop a multi-generational community committed to *GLORIFYING* God, *GROWING* in Christ, and *GOING* with the Gospel.

This vision has shaped the congregation into a truly missional church. They are reaching their "Jerusalem" through outreach in West Columbia, their "Judea" through ministry across South Carolina, their "Samaria" through church planting partnerships in Portland (OR), and the "uttermost parts of the world" through ongoing missions in Ukraine.

The "Missional" Church reminds us that renewal is not complete until it turns outward. A renewed church is a sending church—one that carries the Gospel from its own community to the nations, for the glory of God.

Reflection Questions

1. Is your church currently more focused inward or outward? Why?

_____

_____

2. What local needs exist that your church could meet this year?

_____

_____

3. Who are five people you are praying will come to Christ?

_____

_____

Closing Prayer

Lord, we stand in Your strength. Send us in Your love. Forgive us for living safe and silent. Open our eyes to the lost, the broken, the waiting. Let our church not be a monument, but a movement—fueled by Your Spirit and shaped by Your mission. Let our feet go where Your heart beats. In Jesus' name. Amen

Chapter 9

The Legacy Church
When One Generation Breathes for the Next

Key Text: 2 Timothy 2:2
"And what you have heard from me in the presence of many witnesses entrust to faithful men, who will be able to teach others also."

A Church Story: The "Need Help" Church

The "Need Help" Church was planted in 1985 in a growing suburban area of the metro. She thrived in her early years. But after a series of difficult transitions, the congregation dwindled to just fourteen members. The people had asked for help from sister churches before, but this time their voices carried the weight of weariness. They asked again, *"Is there a church out there that will help us?"* I sensed desperation this time, so my reply was simply, *"Yes. Let me get back with you."*

A few days later, I spoke with the pastor of The "Helping" Church, a sister church in the area. He agreed to meet with the group, and in that first gathering, he wisely asked each of the twelve members present to share how they had come to faith in Christ. It was a powerful reminder of their roots in the Gospel. Afterward, he explained what a partnership with The "Helping" Church would look like.

The following Sunday, The "Need Help" Church announced a special called meeting to consider disbanding and giving their property and buildings (and debt) to The "Helping" Church for the purpose of advancing the Gospel at that location. In the weeks that followed, the membership voted unanimously to continue their legacy of disciple-making through the launch of The "Helping" Church *West*— a thriving replant born out of a dying church.

Today, some of the former members of The "Need Help" Church still worship at The "Helping" Church West. Their legacy carried forward as part of a new season of life and mission.

This story reminds us that even when a chapter closes, God is writing new beginnings for the sake of the Gospel.

The Real Challenge Is Sustaining

Renewal is a beautiful beginning—but it was never meant to be the end. Many churches catch a spark: people return, worship deepens, baptisms rise, and hope begins to stir again. But the true measure of renewal isn't found in a single season of momentum—it's found in the quiet faithfulness that follows. The real challenge isn't starting; it's continuing. Sustaining spiritual vitality requires more than emotion—it takes a new way of life. A church that truly breathes is one that learns to inhale the presence of the Spirit and exhale the mission of the Gospel—day after day, year after year.

Renewal is never meant to be a fleeting moment—it's meant to plant roots for a lasting movement. In Deuteronomy 6, God makes His heart clear: His desire is not only that His people love Him passionately, but that they *pass it on intentionally.*

> *"You shall teach them diligently to your children... talk of them when you sit... bind them... write them..."*
> (Deut. 6:7-9)

This is the language of legacy—not just renewal. True spiritual renewal doesn't end with one generation celebrating; it continues with the next generation walking in truth.

A church that breathes the life of God doesn't always grow bigger, but she always grows deeper. She matures generationally. She raises up sons and daughters in the faith. She disciples parents, grandparents, and children alike—not with hype, but with holy habits that endure.

Renewal may start with fire, but legacy is built with faithfulness. And that is what God is after.

How to Become a Church That Keeps Breathing

Breathing churches are not defined by one great moment of renewal—they're marked by a sustained movement of the Spirit over time. They don't just come alive once; they keep living, keep growing, and keep going. They know that renewal is not a one-time event—it's a culture. Becoming a church that doesn't just breathe again, but keeps breathing for generations, begins with a culture of discipleship.

1. Multiply Disciples

A church that breathes deeply is one that multiplies disciples, not just celebrates decisions. True transformation doesn't stop at conversion—it continues through intentional, everyday obedience to Jesus. That means equipping people to follow Christ in the real, ordinary rhythms of life. It means prioritizing heart change over mere behavior change and creating clear, relational pathways for growth through biblical teaching, mentoring, and small groups that foster spiritual maturity. In churches like this, it becomes normal— even expected—to ask: "Who are you discipling?" and "Who is discipling you?" Jesus' command to "Go and make disciples" was not a suggestion for a few—it's a calling for every church, in every generation.

2. Invest in Leadership Development

Sustainable churches also invest in leadership development. Paul's instruction to Timothy in 2 Timothy 2:2 is a blueprint for sustainable ministry: *"Entrust what you've heard to faithful people who will be able to teach others also."* That's four generations of leaders in one verse. Breathing churches look ahead. They identify potential, develop character, and multiply vision. They don't just delegate tasks—they develop people. They mentor emerging leaders, create safe spaces for them to grow, and give them real responsibility and room to fail with grace. The goal isn't to build followers of leaders—but leaders of others. When you invest in leaders, you're investing in legacy.

3. Celebrate God's Faithfulness

Healthy churches also document and celebrate God's faithfulness. Never let the miracle become a memory. Tell the story of what God has done in your church. Record it. Share testimonies. Create space for people to speak of answered prayers, salvations, and breakthroughs. In Joshua 4, after Israel crossed the Jordan, God told them to build a memorial out of stones—so that when future generations asked, "What do these stones mean?" they would remember God's power and presence. Likewise, if we don't celebrate and share the story of renewal, the next generation may assume church is just routine. Your church's story is not just history—it's fuel for the future.

4. Prioritize Simple Rhythms

Establishing healthy rhythms is essential. Churches don't lose their breath from lack of passion—they lose it from unsustainable pace. Instead of over-programming, breathing churches prioritize simple, consistent rhythms that keep them aligned with the Spirit—monthly gatherings for prayer and worship, weekly small group discipleship, regular year-round outreach, and annual strategic reviews for realignment and vision. These churches don't wait for burnout or crisis to reflect—they realign regularly, knowing that the health of the body depends on the rhythm of its breath.

5. Guard Culture Fiercely

Finally, they guard the culture fiercely. Culture is the soul of the church—it shapes everything. And it always drifts unless it's guarded. Breathing churches define their core values clearly and revisit them often. They say them. Display them. Live them. They allow their values to shape decisions, budgets, calendars, and leadership pipelines. They affirm that prayer is our first response, people matter more than programs, the Spirit leads—not preferences, every member is a missionary, and truth is spoken in love. These values are taught to new members, reaffirmed with teams, and celebrated when lived out. When you guard the culture, you protect the breath—and the body keeps standing strong.

A Church Story: The "Discipler" Church

The "Discipler" Church emerged from a season of tiredness, weariness, and even brokenness. Their pastor described it as a wake-up call: he realized that no single leader could carry the full weight of the local church. Instead of trying to do it all himself, he embraced a new conviction—that the health of the church depends on equipping the saints for the work of ministry.

He began to transfer truth, faithfully grounding his people in God's Word, not just from the pulpit but in one-on-one and small-group settings. He worked to elevate discipleship, making it the heartbeat of the church's mission rather than an optional program. Along the way, he encouraged the congregation to celebrate holy moments— baptisms, reconciliations, answered prayers, and simple steps of obedience—as visible reminders that God was at work among them.

The vision reached into homes as well. The pastor urged families to disciple in the home, teaching parents and grandparents that the front lines of discipleship often begin around a dinner table or bedtime prayer. At the same time, he reminded the church to invest in long-term ministry, building patiently rather than chasing quick results, trusting that God honors steady faithfulness over time.

Above all, he modeled and taught a reliance on the Holy Spirit for wisdom in leadership, power in preaching, and transformation in lives. His consistent message was clear: strategies may help, but only the Spirit gives life.

Today, The "Discipler" Church is growing both deeper and larger. Their story reminds us that renewal does not come by charisma or programs, but by a community that equips its people, multiplies disciples, and trusts the Spirit to breathe life into every generation.

How to Build a Culture of Legacy

Legacy doesn't happen by accident—it's cultivated with intention. A legacy-building church doesn't just celebrate spiritual moments; it creates spiritual milestones. It doesn't just reach the next generation—it disciples them with depth and direction.

1. Equip to Transfer Truth

To shape that kind of culture, we begin by teaching with transfer in mind. It's not enough to inspire; we must equip. Preaching and teaching should help people pass truth on to others. Churches must create environments where families, small groups, and ministry teams not only hear the Word but talk about how they're living it out in daily life.

2. Elevate Discipleship

Spiritual depth creates generational strength. That's why discipleship must be elevated over mere attendance. It means investing in clear, intentional pathways that raise up leaders, form character, and build biblical literacy—from children's ministry to senior adults. The goal isn't just to grow a crowd, but to form disciples who can make disciples.

3. Celebrate Holy Moments

Legacy is also marked by celebration. Baptisms, family dedications, graduations, and recommitments are more than just events—they're holy moments that tell the story of God's faithfulness. When churches honor these moments, they help everyone see that legacy is unfolding before their eyes.

4. Disciple in the Home

This kind of culture begins at home. Parents and grandparents are the most consistent disciple-makers a child will ever know. Churches must empower families to talk about faith at the dinner table, to pray together, and to live the Gospel in their everyday rhythms. Legacy begins in the living room, not the sanctuary.

5. Invest in Long-Term Ministry

And while it's easy to be drawn to short-term wins, legacy-building churches invest in long-term ministry. They think in decades, not just days. They build ministries that will outlast them, train future leaders now, and budget with a future generation in mind. They sow seeds they may never personally harvest—but God will.

6. Continual Reliance on the Holy Spirit

At the heart of all this is a continual reliance on the Holy Spirit. Legacy flows from life. When a church stays Spirit-filled and mission-focused, its influence won't stop at the sanctuary doors—it will stretch across generations.

So church, don't settle for a moment when God is inviting you into a movement. The flame He has rekindled in you is not just for today—it's for tomorrow, and the day after, and the generation after that. You are not just called to be revived; you are called to leave a legacy. Teach the next generation. Walk faithfully in front of them. Show them what it means to love Jesus with your whole heart and to live on mission with your whole existence.

The breath God has given you is not only for survival—it's for sending. So, breathe deep, stand tall, and build something that will last beyond you. Because renewal is the spark—but legacy is the fire that keeps burning.

Why Renewal Often Doesn't Last

True renewal is a holy gift—but it must be nurtured to be sustained. Many churches experience a powerful season of renewal only to find themselves slowly slipping back into stagnancy. Why does this happen? It's rarely due to a lack of desire. More often, it's because the systems, priorities, and spiritual rhythms needed to support renewal were never fully built.

1. Leadership Transitions Aren't Prepared For

One of the primary reasons renewal fades is that leadership transitions are not adequately prepared for. When renewal is tied too closely to a single leader, everything can unravel when that leader steps away. Momentum fades, vision stalls, and the church struggles to find its footing. Sustaining renewal requires shared leadership, intentional succession planning, and a culture that outlives any one individual.

2. Mission Drift Returns

Another challenge is that mission drift returns. After the excitement of renewal, it's tempting to coast. As comfort sets in, urgency slips away. The focus gradually shifts from God's purposes to our own preferences. To stay alive, a church must keep mission at the center—repeatedly asking, "Are we still aligned with the heart of God?"

3. No Pathways to Discipleship

In many cases, no discipleship pathways exist. When people respond to the Gospel but aren't rooted in discipleship, spiritual momentum eventually dries up. Inspiration without formation won't last. Churches need clear, ongoing pathways for spiritual growth—helping new believers mature and longtime members go deeper.

4. Church Forgets Her Story

Sometimes the church forgets her story. Every renewal has a story—but if it's not told, it will be lost. People move on. Staff changes. The miracle fades into memory, and routine takes over. Churches must remember—and retell— their story of renewal. It keeps gratitude fresh and vision alive.

5. Spiritual Rhythms Aren't Reinforced

Perhaps most critically, spiritual rhythms aren't reinforced. No matter how strong a church becomes, it can grow dry again if it neglects its spiritual foundation. Without rhythms of prayer, repentance, worship, and reflection, even vibrant churches lose vitality. Renewal must be sustained by consistent habits of the heart that keep the church rooted in the presence and power of God.

Passing Renewal to the Next Generation

Renewal is powerful—but its greatest impact is seen not just in how it begins, but in whether it continues. A church that experiences renewal has a holy responsibility: to ensure it doesn't end with them. The next generation must not only hear about what God did—they must be invited to experience what God is doing.

1. Include Youth

It begins by including youth in the movement. Don't just give students a seat in the sanctuary—give them a place in the story. Let them experience the presence and power of the Spirit firsthand. Invite them to lead in prayer, serve in visible roles, and speak into real ministry conversations. Create intergenerational moments—testimonies, prayer gatherings, service projects—where wisdom is passed from the seasoned to the seeking. Affirm the voice and energy of young leaders without compromising biblical truth or spiritual maturity. If they see renewal lived—not just talked about—they'll begin to own it for themselves.

2. Refuse to Idolize the Past

Next, refuse to idolize the past. Honoring the past is good. Idolizing it is dangerous. When churches become museums of what was, they forfeit the opportunity to shape what could be. Celebrate the faithfulness of earlier generations—but teach the next generation that God is not done. The best stories aren't just behind us—they're unfolding now. Lift their eyes to see that the God of the past is still the God of the present—and the future. You cannot pass on renewal if your only language is nostalgia.

3. Trust the Spirit

And above all, trust the Spirit to sustain what He began. You are not responsible for manufacturing lasting renewal—you're called to steward it. Philippians 1:6 reminds us, *"He who began a good work in you will carry it on to completion until the day of Christ Jesus."* That means your job is faithfulness. Stay humble. Stay dependent. Stay yielded to the Spirit who started the work. Teach the next generation to build on a foundation of surrender—not strategy. When the church models dependence more than performance, the next generation learns that power comes not from us, but from the Spirit who breathes life into dry bones again and again.

To the next generation—this is your time. You are not just the future of the church; you are part of what God is doing *right now.* You were born into this moment with purpose, filled with potential, and called to walk in the same power that raised Jesus from the dead. You don't need to copy the past—you need to carry the mission forward.

So don't wait to be invited—step in. Ask questions. Seek wisdom. Pray bold prayers. Take responsibility for your faith and your generation. The church needs your voice, your fire, your love for Jesus, and your willingness to go where others may hesitate. Let God breathe through you and let the world see that the Gospel is still alive in your hands.

This is the vision—not just renewal for a season, but sustained renewal for a generation. The Church that breathes is not dependent on trends, personalities, or perfect conditions. She is rooted in the unchanging Gospel, fueled by the Holy Spirit, and committed to living on mission in every season.

Long after the founding leaders have passed the baton, a breathing church continues to rise. She still proclaims Christ. She still welcomes the lost. It still makes disciples. It still sends leaders. She still lives in rhythm with the Spirit of God.

This is not just a comeback story. It's a legacy. Not just a renewal. A movement. A church that breathes—even in a changing world—can be the Church that changes the world.

A Church Story: The "Legacy" Church

Northwood Baptist Church was once located on one of the busiest roads in Lexington County, South Carolina. For years, the congregation prayed, invited, and worked hard to grow, but they struggled to reach young families. As the membership aged, the challenge only grew greater.

At the appropriate time, I spoke with the leadership about becoming a *legacy church*—a church willing to invest its resources so that other churches could be planted, some

174

replanted, and others renewed to reach future generations with the Gospel. The Northwood congregation embraced that vision and donated their 17 acres of prime property to their local Baptist association, allowing for a new church to be planted on the site. In addition, from the sale of a second property the church owned, they established an endowment for their local Baptist association to use for funding church planting, replanting, and revitalization efforts around the world.

The endowment was established at the Baptist Foundation of South Carolina as *the Northwood Baptist Church Legacy Endowment Fund,* with an initial contribution of $10,000. Within a few years, when the second piece of property is sold, the church will deposit the proceeds into the endowment, which is expected to grow to nearly $800,000—an investment that will resource Gospel work for generations to come.

Northwood Baptist Church continues to meet today in available space at their local Baptist association.

Northwood's story reminds us that even when a church cannot see its own path forward, when she entrusts her future to the Gospel, her legacy can bear fruit for generations.... all for the glory of God.

Reflection Questions

1. What spiritual rhythms in your church are sustainable long-term? What needs rethinking?

2. How are you preparing leaders who can carry the mission forward when current leaders step aside?

3. What systems are in place to ensure discipleship continues in the next generation?

Closing Prayer

Lord, thank You for reviving what was once dry. But don't let it stop here. Teach us to breathe again and again. Give us wisdom to prepare the next generation, courage to remain faithful, and joy in the journey. Make our churches flames that do not burn out. Let the breath You gave us become a legacy of life for those who follow. In Jesus' name, Amen

Chapter 10

A Call to a New Beginning
The Final Call—A New Beginning

Key Text: Ezekiel 37:10
"So I prophesied as He commanded me, and the breath came into them, and they lived and stood on their feet, an exceedingly great army."

A Church Story: The "Renaissance" Church

The "Renaissance" Church, located in a rural area of the state, had reached a breaking point. For decades, the sanctuary had echoed with hymns sung by children, laughter in the hallways, and the sound of doors swinging open to welcome neighbors. However, in recent years, the pews grew emptier, the baptistry stayed dry, and the joy of fellowship had given way to fatigue and quiet resignation. A faithful remnant remained, clinging to hope but silently wondering if the end was near.

When I first met with them, the mood was heavy. The conversation in their hearts was a significant concern about their future. *I don't know if we have a future* was the sentiment without saying it. Some later stated the renewal process was like a "last call"—one final chance before the doors might close.

But God delights in final calls, because with Him, endings often mark the beginning of resurrection.

Together, the church began to pray like never before. They returned to the Gospel as their foundation and to prayer as their lifeline. Members began confessing hurts, reconciling relationships, and daring to dream that God might not be finished with them after all.

Then it happened. The worship services were fuller, the singing stronger, the prayers bolder, new believers stepping forward seeking to follow Christ in baptism—six adults and a teenager on one Sunday. The Spirit was breathing in the church again.

What once felt like the final call was now a new beginning.

The valley of dry bones had begun to rattle, and breath had returned. God had written a new chapter: a church that breathes again, rising from the edge of death into a future alive with His glory.

Dry Bones No More

The valley is quiet no longer. What was once filled with brittle remnants of the past—scattered, silent, and sun-bleached by time—is now rumbling with resurrection.

The bones are not abandoned.

They are assembled. They are awakened. They are alive. The breath of God has entered where despair once ruled. This is not a metaphor for long ago. This is a divine declaration for today. It is not reserved for the golden years of the early church or the modern models of innovation. This is a word for the forgotten congregation on the edge of town. For the pastor who wonders if he has anything left to give. For the praying remnant that refuses to quit. For the church that dares to believe that its best days are not behind it. If God can raise an army from a valley of bones, He can raise a revival from a pew of the faithful. This is your moment. Dry bones no more. The Spirit is calling.

The Vision Has Always Been Resurrection

From beginning to end, the vision has never changed. The heart of God beats with resurrection. From Genesis to Revelation, the story of Scripture is a divine movement from death to life—again and again. In Eden, breath was first given. In the wilderness, manna fell. In the valley, bones rattled. In the tomb, the stone rolled. It's not just a series of miracles—it's the very nature of God. He brings life where death has claimed victory.

Abraham's aging frame was quickened by promise, and he became the father of nations. Israel's chains were shattered, and the breath of deliverance carried them through the sea. Jesus stepped into death and came out carrying resurrection in His hands. At Pentecost, the Spirit didn't just fill a room—He filled a people. Flames danced, languages erupted, and the Church was born, not with strategy but with Spirit.

And still today, God is breathing. Not into lifeless routines or polished programs. Not into nostalgic memories or institutional pride. He is breathing into people. Into saints hungry for more. Into weary pastors who haven't given up. Into congregations who dare to believe He is not finished yet. He breathes not into buildings, but into bodies, not into history, but into hope. This is not just what God has done— it is what He *still* does.

Resurrection isn't the ending of the story. It's the rhythm of the Church. And it's still happening.

You're Standing in a Story That Is Not Over

Some churches are beginning to realize: their story isn't over—it's just entering a new chapter. The signs of decline aren't the end; they're the setting for a fresh move of God. Instead of saying, *"We've had our day,"* faithful voices are rising to say, *"God's not finished with us yet."* Rather than believing *"young people don't come here anymore,"* churches are opening their arms and preparing the way for the next generation. Instead of thinking *"this community is too far gone,"* they're proclaiming,

"This is fertile ground for revival."

Because here's the truth: the bones may have been dry, but they are not beyond breath. The Spirit is still moving.

The Savior is still building. The promise of Jesus still stands:

> *"...I will build My Church, and the gates of hell shall not prevail against it."* Matthew 16:18b

You are not standing in a graveyard. You are standing in a garden—one that Heaven is watering again. You are not witnessing the final act. You are watching the Author write a new one. He is not finished with your church, your community, or your calling. The best days of the Church are not behind us—they are rising with resurrection power. So, lift your eyes. Strengthen your hands. Stand in hope. You are part of a story that Heaven is still telling.

God's Army Rises from Ashes, Not Comfort

When the Spirit of God moves, He doesn't just renew—He mobilizes. Ezekiel declared,

> *"...they lived and stood on their feet, an exceedingly great army."* Ezekiel 37:10b

Not a committee, not a crowd, not a tradition—but an army. That's what happens when God breathes: ordinary people rise with extraordinary purpose.

God never intended for His Church to simply survive in safety. He designed us to thrive in Spirit-filled courage. The same Spirit who raised Jesus from the dead now lives in us—

and He is calling us forward. We were not created for comfort but for Kingdom impact. Not to sit in silence, but to stand in strength.

This is not a battle against people—it's a calling to bring light into darkness. As Paul reminds us,

"...we do not wrestle against flesh and blood..."
Ephesians 6:12a

We are here not to retreat but to restore, not to criticize but to carry hope. The Church empowered by the Spirit is not loud with noise but strong in love, grace, and truth.

And that's exactly what the world is longing for—not another polished performance, but a genuine, joyful, Spirit-empowered people. A Church that breathes in the presence of God and breathes out the hope of Christ. A Church that rises with compassion, walks in unity, serves with boldness, and carries Good News to the ends of the earth.

So, take heart—God is raising up an army of faith, formed not in ease, but in encounter. Forged not in comfort, but in calling. Your church is not forgotten. You are not finished. The breath of God is stirring again—and you are being raised, not just to stand, but to shine.

A Church Story: "New Beginning" Church

The "New Beginning" Church is in a demographically changing community. She has a long history of a thriving ministry in her community. But over the past twenty-five years, the congregation has faced difficult transitions and ongoing challenges. Many members no longer live in the community, which has shifted from predominantly white families to a growing Hispanic, African American, and college student population.

In recent years, the church entered a renewal process that helped bring stability. Under the leadership of their pastor—faithful in the pulpit, passionate about reaching people, and sacrificial in his commitment—the congregation has sought to adapt and embrace its mission.

While growth has been slow, signs of life are emerging. Several new believers have come to faith and requested baptism. Others have joined the fellowship. Members are stepping up to serve. There is no conflict, only a renewed spirit of hope.

What some once expressed concern as the closing of a chapter now appears to be the beginning of a new one...all for His glory!

The "New Beginning" Church is learning that even after years of difficulty, God can spark fresh beginnings in a church that remains faithful and open to His Spirit.

Let the Wind Blow Again

The great prayer of Ezekiel 37:9 still echoes through the valley of today's Church:

"...Come from the four winds, O breath, and breathe on these slain, that they may live." Ezekiel 37:9b

That cry is not ancient history—it is our present hope. It is the heart-cry of pastors weary in the trenches, of churches longing to see life again, of believers aching for something more than routine.

WRITE YOUR CHURCH STORY

Even now, as you read these words, your church's story is being written. The question is—what will that story tell?

_____

_____

_____

_____

_____

_____

_____

_____

_____

_____

END NOTES

1. *Growing Young: Six Essential Strategies to Help Young People Discover and Love Your Church* – by Kara Powell, Jake Mulder, and Brad Griffin (Fuller Youth Institute).

2. *Autopsy of a Deceased Church: 12 Ways to Keep Yours Alive* – by Thom S. Rainer.

3. *Didn't See It Coming: Overcoming the Seven Greatest Challenges That No One Expects and Everyone Experiences* – by Carey Nieuwhof.

4. *Forgotten God: Reversing Our Tragic Neglect of the Holy Spirit* was authored by Francis Chan (with Danae Yankoski as a contributing writer).

Acknowledgements

Suggested Reading & Influences

The truths explored in *Breath to the Bones* have been deeply shaped by Scripture, personal ministry experience, and the wisdom of many faithful leaders who have poured their lives into the local church. While this book is not a direct commentary on any one author's work, I gratefully acknowledge the influence of the following writers, pastors, and thinkers whose voices echo in these pages:

- **Mark Clifton** – *Reclaiming Glory: Revitalizing Dying Churches*
  His clear voice on church replanting has deeply shaped the way many of us think about dying churches and resurrection hope.
- **Thom Rainer** – *Autopsy of a Deceased Church*
  A sobering, research-based look at patterns of decline that often mirror what we experience on the ground.
- **Tim Keller** – *Center Church* and *The Prodigal God*
  His emphasis on Gospel centrality, city-focused ministry, and grace-fueled transformation has profoundly shaped the church renewal conversation.

- **Ed Stetzer** – Thought leader in church planting and revitalization, with extensive insight into cultural engagement and mission.
- **J.D. Greear** – *Gaining by Losing* and *Jesus,* A fresh call to prioritize the sending nature of the church and the active work of the Holy Spirit in everyday ministry.
- **Henry and Richard Blackaby** – *Experiencing God* Their writing has shaped how many leaders view God's activity in the church and how to join Him in it.
- **Leonard Sweet** – *Soul Tsunami* and *Aqua Church* His prophetic edge and poetic insights into the postmodern church challenge us to reimagine without compromising the core.
- **Eugene Peterson** – *The Pastor: A Memoir* A reminder of the long obedience and pastoral faithfulness behind every true story of revitalization.

These voices, along with countless unnamed mentors, missionaries, professors, and faithful church members, have influenced my thinking and stirred my soul. I offer this work in the same spirit of humility and hope—that the Church might live again, fully awake, fully alive, and fully centered on the Gospel of Jesus Christ.

ABOUT THE AUTHOR

Johnny Rumbough served nearly three decades (1996–2025) as the Executive Director/Associational Mission Strategist of the Lexington Baptist Association in South Carolina. Before that, he was appointed by the North American Mission Board to serve at the Greenville Baptist Association (1991–1996) and was earlier appointed by the North American Mission Board to plant a church in Tega Cay, SC (1985–1990).

He is a graduate of Charleston Southern University (1981) and earned a Master of Divinity from Southwestern Baptist Theological Seminary (1985). In recognition of his leadership and service, Charleston Southern University awarded him an honorary Doctor of Religion degree in 2003.

Across five decades of ministry, Johnny has spoken in hundreds of churches and on numerous platforms. He has served congregations of varying sizes as senior pastor, associate pastor, and interim pastor. He has planted two churches, replanted three, and led dozens through a renewal process. He has trained more than 180 pastor search committees and guided many churches and associations through seasons of renewal and revitalization.

Most importantly, Johnny came to faith in Christ in 1975 and married his wife, Valerie (English), the following year. Together they have two children—Jason (Kelli) and Jamie (Justin)—and six grandchildren: Micah, Luka, Noelle, Liam, Judah, and Charlotte. They make their home in Chapin, South Carolina.